Mezzo-Soprano/Belter V

The Singers Musical Theatre Anthology

A collection of songs from the musical stage, categorized by voice type. The selections are presented in their authentic settings, excerpted from the original vocal scores.

Compiled and Edited by Richard Walters

ISBN-13: 978-1-4234-4699-6
ISBN-10: 1-4234-4699-2

Copyright © 2008 by HAL LEONARD CORPORATION
International Copyright Secured   All Rights Reserved

HAL•LEONARD® CORPORATION

7777 W. BLUEMOUND RD. P.O. BOX 13819 MILWAUKEE, WI 53213

For all works contained herein:
Unauthorized copying, arranging, adapting, recording or public performance is an infringement of copyright.
Infringers are liable under the law.

Visit Hal Leonard Online at
www.halleonard.com

Foreword

Volume 5 of *The Singer's Musical Theatre Anthology* applies the approach of all past volumes in the series, the first of which were published in 1987. These books represent extensive research of available material, always juggling a mixture of objectives and aims. Those aims are:

- ***To provide an interesting variety of musical theatre literature for an assortment of tastes and talents.***

Individual and editorial tastes admittedly and inescapably play a part in the compilations, but we deliberately attempt to consider the broader preferences and needs of the thousands of singers, actors and teachers who use these books. What are the needs of the 17-year-old studying voice? Or the 25-year-old female or male ingénue? Or the 40-year-old moving beyond ingénue roles? What about someone looking for pop/rock style theatre music? We try to consider the character actor-singer as well as the handsome-voiced leading man; those with expansive vocal gifts, and those with limited singing voices; comic songs, charm songs, and dramatic songs; young tastes, as well as more mature tastes; singers who are sophisticated musicians, and those who are less musically advanced. The singers who use these volumes range in age from teens to senior citizens. We try to imagine as many of them as possible in choosing songs.

- ***To deliberately represent songs from various eras and styles.***

While it is important to stay current and mine songs from contemporary shows, it is equally important to continue to delve deeper into our shared heritage of theatre music. We have sometimes encountered young musical theatre enthusiasts who only know the latest shows, and have never heard of *Carousel* or *The Most Happy Fella*. We are equally perplexed when speaking with voice teachers or singers whose knowledge of musical theatre seems to end with *Hello, Dolly!* Both perspectives are obviously limited.

- ***Beyond the most prominent songs, also to present intriguing songs that are not often encountered in other collections, and may not be available elsewhere in print.***

Only by working through entire scores of musicals, usually also studying cast albums as well, do we discover less obvious songs which otherwise might not have made it onto the contents lists. A song is not worthy of attention solely because it is obscure, of course. But finding valuable songs that may have been forgotten by most, or never known, is one of the riches of the series.

- ***To present the music in a responsible, faithful edition.***

Standard piano/vocal (or piano/vocal/guitar) sheet music has long been the general format for theatre music, and is an important way for songs to be available for the widest possible uses, including millions of amateur pianists. But these sheet music editions—simplified, often transposed, and usually with the melody in the piano part—are often not the best source for a singing actor. In this series we attempt to present the music as it was originally performed in the first theatrical production, in the original keys, allowing for necessary and practical adjustments in creating an edition of the song. We also provide succinct information about the show, and enough plot synopsis to inform comprehension of the song.

- ***To categorize songs by voice type for practical use.***

Musical theatre is often not composed with traditional voice types in mind. It is sometimes tricky business deciding whether any given song belongs in the soprano or belter volume, or in the tenor or baritone/bass volume. The vocal range of a song only tells part of the story. What is the predominant area of the voice (called the *tessitura*) in the song? What is the vocal timbre that the song seems to require? What type of voice is on the original cast recording?

Categorizing songs sung by sopranos who also belt is one of the most challenging aspects of the task. This is a different voice type from the naturally lower, more sultry voice that predominantly belts; or a voice of more limited range; or the brassier timbre that has little usable head voice. It is common for a musical theatre role to call for both soprano singing and belting, often times with a mix of approaches within the same song. These parts are usually cast with sopranos who also can belt; at its best it is a natural, unforced belt that is simply part of the vocal equipment of the singer well-suited to musical theatre.

In choosing songs for the soprano volume, we took into consideration whether the singer on the cast album is a soprano, even though she may be belting at times. Kristin Chenoweth is a good example of a soprano who can easily belt, depending on the character and range of the material and how she wants it to sound. Christine Ebersole is also such a singer. Clearly, she is a soprano, and even though her Act II material in *Grey Gardens* calls for some belting, her vocal instrument still functions as a soprano who belts. Sutton Foster is another current performer whose voice is essentially a soprano that sometimes also belts. At times the choice about where to place songs in *The Singer's Musical Theatre Anthology* seems impossible, and compromise is inevitable. For Christine's songs from *Dirty Rotten Scoundrels* (originally sung by Sherie René Scott), the solution was to put one in the soprano volume, and the other in the mezzo-soprano/belter volume, even though they are both sung by the same singer. We make the best judgments possible and know that there is sometimes room for other conclusions.

- ***Overall, to continue to value musical theatre as a body of vocal literature.***

Musical theatre is a respectable body of literature that deserves the same consideration as novels, poetry, plays, symphonies, operas, or any composed and deliberately conceived work.

And, by the way, beyond being a wealth of literature deserving high-minded study, musical theatre is also fun, of course. Here's to having some fun with the songs in this collection.

A four-volume series can't be done alone. I thank Chris Ruck and Joel Boyd for their aid in preparing the music pages for publication. Michael Dansicker was always ready with ideas and musical sources, and I thank him for his interest and help. Some of the composers were gracious in their accommodations. Most of all, I would like to thank assistant editor Brian Dean for his enthusiastic work on "Volume 5." Without him, you would not be holding this book in your hands.

Richard Walters
Editor
January, 2008

THE SINGER'S MUSICAL THEATRE ANTHOLOGY
Mezzo-Soprano/Belter Volume 5

Contents

THE ACT
14 City Lights

AIN'T MISBEHAVIN'
24 Keepin' Out of Mischief Now

AVENUE Q
29 Special

THE BAKER'S WIFE
34 Meadowlark

BARNUM
49 The Colors of My Life

BELLS ARE RINGING
52 It's a Perfect Relationship

CHILDREN OF EDEN
66 Children of Eden

CITY OF ANGELS
59 What You Don't Know About Women

THE COLOR PURPLE
70 Too Beautiful for Words

CURTAINS
84 Thinking of Him
73 It's a Business

DIRTY ROTTEN SCOUNDRELS
88 Here I Am

DREAMGIRLS
95 And I Am Telling You I'm Not Going
104 I Am Changing

THE DROWSY CHAPERONE
110 Show Off

GREASE
118 Freddy, My Love

GREY GARDENS
125 The Cake I Had

HAIRSPRAY
132 Good Morning Baltimore

THE LAST FIVE YEARS
139 When You Come Home to Me
150 I Can Do Better than That

THE LIFE
162 My Body

A LITTLE PRINCESS
170 Live Out Loud

MAMMA MIA!
178 The Winner Takes It All

ON A CLEAR DAY YOU CAN SEE FOREVER
188 Hurry! It's Lovely Up Here

THE PIRATE QUEEN
194 Woman

RENT
208 Without You

SONG AND DANCE
201 Take That Look Off Your Face

SOPHISTICATED LADIES
218 Hit Me with a Hot Note

MONTY PYTHON'S SPAMALOT
223 Find Your Grail

SPRING AWAKENING
236 Mama Who Bore Me
228 The Dark I Know Well

SWEET CHARITY
244 If My Friends Could See Me Now
239 Where Am I Going

TARZAN
252 You'll Be in My Heart

THOROUGHLY MODERN MILLIE
257 Not for the Life of Me

TICK, TICK...BOOM!
264 Come to Your Senses

WICKED
272 Defying Gravity
282 For Good

WORKING
291 It's an Art

ZORBA
306 Life Is

ABOUT THE SHOWS

THE ACT

MUSIC: John Kander
LYRICS: Fred Ebb
BOOK: George Furth
DIRECTOR: Martin Scorsese
CHOREOGRAPHER: Ron Lewis
OPENED: October, 28, 1977, New York; a run of 233 performances

A star vehicle written by Kander and Ebb for Liza Minnelli, *The Act* was about a legendary performer, Michelle Craig (Liza) a movie star trying to make a comeback with a nightclub act on stage at the Hotel Las Vegas. There was very little plot; it was mostly a showcase for Liza, who won the 1978 Tony Award as Best Actress in a Musical for her work in the show. Though it set a record for highest ticket price and had the biggest pre-sale in Broadway history to that date, the run was marred by Ms. Minnelli's frequent absences. The song **"City Lights"** opened the second act of *The Act*.

AIN'T MISBEHAVIN'

MUSIC: Thomas "Fats" Waller
LYRICS: Various writers
CONCEPT: Murray Horowitz and Richard Maltby, Jr.
DIRECTOR: Richard Maltby, Jr.
CHOREOGRAPHER: Arthur Faria
OPENED: March 9, 1978, New York; a run of 1,604 performances

This hit show set a trend for the return of the plotless revue to Broadway. *Ain't Misbehavin'* features music by pianist and composer Thomas Wright "Fats" Waller (1904-1943), considered the greatest player of the stride piano style. Waller died young of pneumonia, possibly more susceptible due to his weight and drinking. The revue began as a limited-run cabaret entertainment of at the Manhattan Theatre Club in February, 1978. Its enthusiastic reception prompted a transfer to Broadway. Among the numbers performed were 18 written by Waller (some as instrumental pieces, with new lyrics by Richard Maltby, Jr. and Murray Horowitz), and 12 other songs recorded by Waller. Through costuming, décor, and arrangements, the original production evoked the flavor of a Harlem nightclub in the 1930s, with the playful spirit of Waller himself coming through in the performance. A Broadway revival opened in 1988.

AVENUE Q

MUSIC AND LYRICS: Robert Lopez and Jeff Marx
BOOK: Jeff Whitty
DIRECTOR: Jason Moore
CHOREOGRAPHER: Ken Roberson
OPENED: July 31, 2003, New York

Avenue Q, which first played Off-Broadway in 2002, is an ironic homage to "Sesame Street," though the puppet characters are decidedly adult, dealing with topics such as loud lovemaking, closeted homosexuality, and internet porn addiction. The puppeteers visibly are onstage, acting and singing for their characters, and there are video clips too. The story deals with a young college graduate, Princeton, who seeks his purpose in life and looks for love. Along the way we meet the many tenants in his apartment building on the rundown Avenue Q, in an outer borough of New York. **"Special"** is sung by Lucy the Slut in Act I in a stage-within-a-stage scene at the Around the Clock Cafe. Lucy comes on to Princeton, seduces him and tries to sabotage a budding relationship he has with Kate, who throws a penny from the top of the Empire State Building that hits Lucy in the head and puts her into a coma.

These notes are principally by the editor, with occasional writing by Stanley Green excerpted from Broadway Musicals Show by Show, *published by Hal Leonard.*

THE BAKER'S WIFE

MUSIC AND LYRICS: Stephen Schwartz
BOOK: Joseph Stein

In the 1950s Frank Loesser was originally to have written a musical based on the 1938 French film *La Femme du Boulanger*. Producer David Merrick later acquired the rights, and with a score by Stephen Schwartz *The Baker's Wife* toured out of town for the unusually long period of six months, but was closed by the writers and producers before making it to Broadway. To the delight of the villagers of the previously bakerless town of Boulanger in Provence in the 1930s, a jolly new baker, the middle-aged Aimable Castagnet (originally played by Paul Sorvino), opens a shop there with his pretty young wife, Geneviève (played by Patti LuPone). She struggles with memories of past loves, but resolves to be a good baker's wife. Her resolve crumbles one evening when she agrees to meet the charming young Dominque an hour later for a late night rendezvous. Before their tryst she considers her feelings and situation in the song **"Meadowlark."** Though she considers staying faithful to her husband (in the song the bird stays with the old king who adored her and perishes), she sets off to meet Dominique. Aimable is despondent and cannot bake, much to the dismay of the villagers. Eventually, Geneviève is brought back to Aimable and the bread-making resumes. *The Baker's Wife* had a brief London run in 1990, and productions continue to pop up here and there.

BARNUM

MUSIC: Cy Coleman
LYRICS: Michael Stewart
BOOK: Mark Bramble
DIRECTOR AND CHOREOGRAPHER: Joe Layton
OPENED: April 30, 1980, New York; a run of 854 performances

This version of the story of America's "Prince of Humbug," Phineas Taylor Barnum, doesn't focus on biography or characterization as much as it offers a circus concept musical. The original production had the cast constantly in motion as they tumbled, clowned, marched, twirled, or flew through the air. Jim Dale was the original Barnum on Broadway, and Glenn Close was his wife Charity (Chairy). Barnum defines "humbug" as simply the puffing up of the truth. The show offers a tour of the highlights of Barnum's career from 1835 to 1880. Throughout, Chairy tries to convince her husband to settle down to a more normal life away from show business. Fairly early in Act I first Barnum sings **"The Colors of My Life,"** with lyrics that are bright and optimistic. Chairy responds with a version of the song with a less rosy, more grounded outlook; her version is used in this authentic show edition for belter. Along the way various acts appear: Tom Thumb, Jumbo the elephant, and Swedish nightingale Jenny Lind, an opera star Barnum presents in her first American concert. Barnum has a dalliance with her and tours with Jenny, leaving his wife for a time. He tires of the demanding diva and returns to Chairy, and agrees to leave show business. After Chairy dies Barnum realizes that a conventional life is not for him, and he makes the deal with James A. Bailey to create "The Greatest Show on Earth" (which after a later merger became Ringling Bros., Barnum & Bailey Circus).

BELLS ARE RINGING

MUSIC: Jule Styne
BOOK AND LYRICS: Betty Comden and Adolph Green
DIRECTOR: Jerome Robbins
CHOREOGRAPHERS: Jerome Robbins and Bob Fosse
OPENED: November 29, 1956, New York; a run of 924 performances

Since appearing with her in a nightclub revue, Comden and Green had wanted to write a musical for their friend, Judy Holliday. The idea they eventually hit upon was to cast Miss Holliday as Ella Peterson, a meddlesome but charming and friendly operator at the Susanswerphone telephone answering service (a now out-of-date type of business later replaced by answering machines, voice mail and cell phones) who gets involved with her clients' lives. She is in fact so helpful to one, a playwright in need of inspiration, that they meet, fall in love (though through it all she conceals her occupation), dance and sing in the subway, and entertain fellow New Yorkers in Central Park. At last she confesses that she's the operator, and after some adjustment they happily couple up. At the top of the show Ella introduces herself, her occupation, and her infatuation with a client she has never met in **"It's a Perfect Relationship."** A film version, directed by Vincent Minelli, was made in 1960 that closely resembles the stage musical, with Dean Martin opposite Miss Holliday. A revival played on Broadway briefly in 2001.

CHILDREN OF EDEN

MUSIC AND LYRICS: Stephen Schwartz
BOOK: John Caird
OPENED: January 8, 1991, London

Loosely based on the Book of Genesis, *Children of Eden* ran in London for three months in 1991, but since then has gained popularity in stock and amateur productions, unusual for a musical without a Broadway run. Schwartz created a revised version of the show in 1997 for the Paper Mill Playhouse, which resulted in a cast recording. After Eve is tempted by eating the forbidden fruit, she and Adam, who chooses to stay with her, are banished from the Garden of Eden. They have two sons, Cain and Abel. Eve realizes that Cain has within him the same restless temptation that caused her to eat the fruit. Cain and Adam argue over the discovery of evidence of other humans. When Abel intervenes, Cain kills him and becomes cursed. As Eve is dying at the end of Act I, she sings **"Children of Eden,"** which expresses her hope that her children and descendants will once again attain the Garden of Eden. Act II tells of Noah, his family and the ark; at the end they long for the lost Garden of Eden.

CITY OF ANGELS

MUSIC: Cy Coleman
LYRICS: David Zippel
BOOK: Larry Gelbart
DIRECTOR: Michael Blakemore
CHOREOGRAPHER: Walter Painter
OPENED: December 11, 1989, New York; a run of 879 performances

City of Angels is a spoof of the hard boiled film noir movies of the 1940s. Stine is a novelist struggling to adapt his mystery novel about fictional Detective Stone into a screenplay. The adventures of Stone come to life as in the musical as Stine writes it. The "real" scenes (with a design reminiscent of black and white movies) with the writer Stine, and his screenplay scenes (evoking color movies) with Stone alternate and interact. Some characters appear in both the "real world" and in the screenplay, with two cast lists: the Hollywood (real world) cast, and the movie cast. Early in Act I Gabby, Stine's wife, tells him an earful in **"What You Don't Know about Women,"** just as Oolie tells Stone the same message in the emerging screenplay. Stine's personal life falls apart later as Gabby accuses him of selling out, and she leaves him. He realizes that he has indeed sold out, and reclaims his values as a man and a writer. *City of Angels* won the 1990 Tony Award for Best Musical, along with Tony Awards in nine other categories.

THE COLOR PURPLE

MUSIC AND LYRICS: Brenda Russell, Allee Willis and Stephen Bray
BOOK: Marsha Norman
DIRECTOR: Gary Griffin
CHOREOGRAPHER: Donald Byrd
OPENED: December 1, 2005, New York

Based on the novel *The Color Purple* by Alice Walker, which was also adapted for a 1985 film, the musical takes place in rural Georgia and later Memphis, 1909 to 1949. Celie has had a hard life, offered at a young age by her father in marriage to a farmer named Mister, who is constantly cruel to her. Celie suffers many hardships as Mister's wife, including being forbidden to see her beloved little sister, Nettie. Shug Avery is a sultry singer and Mister's longtime mistress. She arrives back in town in terrible condition, and despite circumstances, Mister brings Shug home for Celie to nurse. Caring for Shug, Celie realizes for the first time that tender affection can exist between two people. Shug sings **"Too Beautiful for Words"** to the disbelieving but hopeful Celie, telling her that she is graceful, lovely, and desirable. The story continues in Act II and covers many years, with Celie finally leaving Mister, who eventually does change for the better. In the end Celie is finally reunited not only with her sister Nettie, but also with the two children, now adults, taken from her as babies when she was a teenager.

CURTAINS

MUSIC: John Kander
LYRICS: Fred Ebb; additional lyrics by John Kander and Rupert Holmes
BOOK: Rupert Holmes
DIRECTOR: Scott Ellis
CHOREOGRAPHER: Rob Ashford
OPENED: March 22, 2007, New York

Years before it came to Broadway, Kander and Ebb had worked with Peter Stone's original book and concept for what eventually became *Curtains*, but the project was left unfinished. It was picked up again in the new century, with a new book by Rupert Holmes. After Fred Ebb's death in September of 2004, Kander and Holmes also wrote lyrics for the remaining work on the show. This musical comedy is a light-hearted backstage murder mystery set in the Colonial Theatre in Boston, 1959, during the out of town tryout for a mediocre new musical, *Robbin' Hood!*, set in the American West. When its untalented star is murdered during the curtain call on opening night, Lt. Frank Cioffi (David Hyde Pierce in the original cast) of the Boston Police locks down the theatre, confining the entire cast and crew as suspects to be investigated. The colorful characters include the hard-edged producer, Carmen Bernstein (played by Debra Monk in the original cast); her ambitious daughter Bambi (whose real name is Elaine); a split up couple and songwriting team, Aaron and Georgia, still pining for one another; an appealing ingenue; other producers; and the show's director, stage manager, and choreographer/leading man. Frank is in love with the theatre, and finds himself as interested in fixing the show as solving the murder. Along the way he falls for the ingenue. In Act I Georgia Hendricks lets us know how she still feels about her ex in **"Thinking of Him."** Near the top of Act II the tough as nails Carmen sets her daughter, and anyone else within earshot, straight on the financial realities of the theatre in **"It's a Business."**

DIRTY ROTTEN SCOUNDRELS

MUSIC AND LYRICS: David Yazbek
BOOK: Jeffrey Lane
DIRECTOR: Jack O'Brien
CHOREOGRAPHER: Jerry Mitchell
OPENED: March 3, 2005, New York; a run of 627 performances

David Yazbek's follow-up to *The Full Monty* on Broadway (2000) was also based on a notable movie. *Dirty Rotten Scoundrels* takes its name and plot from the 1988 film starring Michael Caine and Steve Martin, which itself was a remake of the 1964 movie *Bedtime Story,* starring David Niven, Marlon Brando and Shirley Jones. The essential story remains the same. Two con men are initially at their game separately, preying upon lonely, wealthy women vacationing on the French Riviera. The suave, British Lawrence Jameson (John Lithgow in the original cast) wines and dines women out of their money, posing as a rich, deposed prince needing funds to fight revolutionaries. Crass American Freddy Benson (Norbert Leo Butz in the original cast) tries to usurp the female fortune through a sob story. When the two grifters meet, they decide that the small town on the French Riviera isn't big enough for both of them. They choose a mark, Christine Colgate (Sherie René Scott in the original cast), the "American Soap Queen." Whoever gets to her money first will get to remain in town. In the end, after many double-crosses, the two scoundrels learn that they're not the only schemers on the French Riviera. Christine swindles them both. Christine introduces herself (or at least who she says she is) as a wide-eyed American provincial girl (laying it on a little thickly) with her entrance song, **"Here I Am."** This role includes both belting and soprano singing; Christine's song "Nothing Is Too Wonderful to Be True" appears in *The Singer's Musical Theatre Anthology, Soprano Volume 5.*

DREAMGIRLS

MUSIC: Henry Krieger
BOOK AND LYRICS: Tom Eyen
DIRECTOR: Michael Bennett
CHOREOGRAPHERS: Michael Bennett, Michael Peters
OPENED: December 20, 1981, New York; a run of 1,521 performances

With *Dreamgirls,* Michael Bennett returned to the heartbreak world of show business that he had explored in *A Chorus Line* to create another high-voltage concept musical. Tom Eyen's tough-tender book about the corruption of innocence of a singing group of the 1960s, The Dreams, was vaguely and loosely a Motown story about the Supremes. Powerhouse voice Effie Melody White (original cast member Jennifer Holliday won a Tony Award for the role), is dropped for the more commercial and simpler lead voice in the group, Deena. There are romantic upsets as well. The trio rises to stardom, and Effie struggles but finally finds a career of her own. The most famous song from the show comes near the end of Act I. **"And I Am Telling You I'm Not Going"** is sung by Effie to Curtis, manager of the group and her boyfriend, after he has fired her and replaced her with another singer. What Curtis does not know is that Effie has missed a few performances because she is having a rough start to a pregnancy with his child. Despite Effie's plea, she does leave the group and moves back home to Chicago. Five difficult years later, now a single mother with a daughter, Effie finally lets go of her anger and begins to find a new attitude and act, shown in the song **"I Am Changing."** A film version of the show was released in 2006; Jennifer Hudson won an Oscar for her performance as Effie.

THE DROWSY CHAPERONE

MUSIC AND LYRICS: Lisa Lambert, Greg Morrison
BOOK: Bob Martin, Don McKellar
DIRECTOR AND CHOREOGRAPHER: Casey Nicholaw
OPENED: May 1, 2006, New York

This show-within-a-show features a rather sour character simply called the Man in Chair, who escapes his depression by obsessively playing an old recording of a 1928 musical, *The Drowsy Chaperone*. Its story is of an actress, Janet Van De Graaff (Sutton Foster in the original cast), indulgent in vanity, engaged to a man she has only recently met. The show, characters, story and songs are an affectionate send-up of stage and screen clichés. Through it all the Man in Chair gets swept up in the action, and comments to the audience. In a song that establishes her character, Janet ironically belts at length that she doesn't want to **"Show Off"** any more. This song and role is for a soprano who can also belt; Janet's other featured solo, "Bride's Lament" is found in *The Singer's Musical Theatre Anthology, Soprano Volume 5*.

GREASE

MUSIC, LYRICS AND BOOK: Jim Jacobs and Warren Casey
DIRECTOR: Tom Moore
CHOREOGRAPHER: Patricia Birch
OPENED: February 14, 1972, New York; a run of 3,388 performances

A surprise runaway hit reflecting the nostalgia fashion of the 1970s, *Grease* is the story Rydell High School students of the late 1950s. Tough Romeo and hip greaser Danny Zuko, his wholesome girl Sandy Dumbrowski, and assorted other characters appear in a light-hearted story, with young love, teen fashions, social cliques, and especially early rock and roll. At a pajama party of the girls gang the Pink Ladies in Act I, Marty has a kimono given to her by Freddy, now in the marines. With others as back-up in the girls group send-up number, Marty sings lead, writing a letter in **"Freddy, My Love."** A Broadway revival opened in 1994 and ran for more than three years; another Broadway revival opened in 2007. The 1978 movie version, starring John Travolta and Olivia Newton-John, is one of the top grossing movie musicals of all time.

GREY GARDENS

MUSIC: Scott Frankel
LYRICS: Michael Korie
BOOK: Doug Wright
DIRECTOR: Michael Greif
CHOREOGRAPHER: Jeff Calhoun
OPENED: November 2, 2006, New York; a run of 308 performances

Grey Gardens, the musical, is based on *Grey Gardens,* the 1975 film documentary, about an eccentric mother and her equally eccentric daughter who remain in a crumbling mansion on Long Island in East Hampton, New York. After a Prologue, Act I of the musical speculates on the past of the principal characters as they were in July, 1941: 47-year-old mother Edith Bouvier Beale, aunt to Jacqueline Bouvier (later Kennedy Onassis), and her 21-year-old daughter Edith "Little Edie" Bouvier Beale. Their mansion home is refined and cultivated. Little Edie is in a relationship with Joseph Kennedy, Jr. (older brother of the president), but her mother sabotages the engagement. In Act II of the musical, set in 1973 and most closely based on the documentary, the 79-year-old Edith (Mary Louise Wilson, who won a Tony Award as Best Featured Actress in a Musical), and her 56-year-old unmarried daughter Little Edie are faded aristocrats living in filth and ruin, isolated from the world, drifting in time. Their relationship is complex and co-dependent. Edith's first song is **"The Cake I Had."** Before it she says, "I have no complaints, I had everything I ever wanted... I had a very happy satisfied life." Little Edie comments, "Can't be done. You can't have your cake and eat it too." Edith replies, "Oh, yes I can. I most certainly did have my cake. And eat it. Down to the last crumb." She then launches into the song. Christine Ebersole won a Tony Award playing Edith in Act I and Little Edie in Act II, and Mary Louise Wilson won a Tony for her portrayal of Edith in Act II.

HAIRSPRAY

MUSIC: Marc Shaiman
LYRICS: Scott Wittman and Marc Shaiman
BOOK: Mark O'Donnell and Thomas Meehan
DIRECTOR: Jack O'Brien
CHOREOGRAPHER: Jerry Mitchell
OPENED: August 15, 2002, New York

Film composer Marc Shaiman helped turn John Waters' campy 1988 movie *Hairspray* into perfect fodder for a new Broadway musical—teenage angst, racial integration, a lot of dancing, and a whole lot of hair. Set in Baltimore, 1962, plump heroine Tracy Turnblad dreams of dancing on local television on the Corny Collins Show, but is upstaged by the prettier, but less talented, current "It-girl" Amber Von Tussle. Tracy gets on the show nonetheless, and gets the attention she craves. She leads efforts to integrate the program, and gains acceptance for all teens of every size, shape and color. The musical opens with Tracy leading the company in **"Good Morning Baltimore,"** in period pop style, starting the day with the sunshine of her personality and her hopes of dancing on TV. The show won the Tony Award for Best Musical in 2003. A film version of the musical was released in 2007.

THE LAST FIVE YEARS

MUSIC, LYRICS AND BOOK: Jason Robert Brown
DIRECTOR: Daisy Prince
OPENED: March 3, 2002, New York

The Off-Broadway musical *The Last Five Years* paired writer Jason Robert Brown and director Daisy Prince together again after their collaboration on the revue *Songs for a New World*. This two-person show chronicles the beginning, middle and deterioration of a relationship between a successful writer and a struggling actress. The show's form is unique. Cathy starts at the end of the relationship, and tells her story backwards, while Jamie starts at the beginning. The only point of intersection is the middle at their engagement. In **"When You Come Home to Me"** Cathy is auditioning in the first section. She obviously hears "thanks" as a signal to stop from the auditioners, and says in reply, "Thank you. Thank you so much." She then expresses herself in a communication to her father. When the audition song starts again, at yet another audition, we hear her inner thoughts as she sings. Near the end of the show, as Cathy's story goes back in time, she sings of her observations about the lives of other young women and hopes for her emerging relationship with Jamie in **"I Can Do Better Than That."** The two original actors Off-Broadway were Norbert Leo Butz and Sherie René Scott.

THE LIFE

MUSIC: Cy Coleman
LYRICS: Ira Gasman
BOOK: David Newman, Ira Gasman, Cy Coleman
DIRECTOR: Michael Blakemore
CHOREOGRAPHER: Joey McKneely
OPENED: April 26, 1997, New York; a run of 466 performances

The Life is set on and around 42nd Street of New York City in the 1980s, when the area before its dramatic revitalization was still the seedy but lively domain of pimps, hookers and topless bars. In Act I the hookers are on the street when a gospel group comes by singing a song. The working girls' lively and defiant response is **"My Body."** The story is of the hard existence on the street, of betrayal, and the hope for a different life.

A LITTLE PRINCESS

MUSIC: Andrew Lippa
LYRICS AND BOOK: Brian Crawley

A Little Princess, based on the novel by Frances Hodgson Burnett, is the story of a little girl with a great big imagination. Separated from her father, and the open-hearted Africans who have helped him raise her, young Sara Crewe is sent to boarding school in London. When things go badly for her there, her imaginative powers come to the rescue helping to transform a drab institution into a place of magic and mystery. Sara sings **"Live Out Loud"** after the cruel headmistress Miss Minchin tries to squelch Sara's high spirits. The musical first played in 2004 in Palo Alto, California.

MAMMA MIA!

MUSIC AND LYRICS: Benny Andersson and Björn Ulvaeus
BOOK: Catherine Johnson
DIRECTOR: Phyllida Lloyd
CHOREOGRAPHER: Anthony Van Laast
OPENED: April 6, 1999, London; October 18, 2001, New York

Mamma Mia! is a "jukebox musical" culled from the catalogue of Swedish pop group ABBA. Over 20 songs are used in the show, more or less in their original form, woven into a libretto created for the stage production. It takes place on a fictional Greek Island where Donna Sheridan runs a small tavern. Her daughter, Sophie, has always wanted to know the identity of her father, but Donna has refused to reveal the information. Sophie sneaks a read of Donna's old diaries, and invites three men from the past, one of whom she believes is possibly her father, to her upcoming wedding. Donna realizes that she still loves one of the men, Sam, though she doesn't want to admit it. It turns out that long ago Sam was having an affair with Donna while being engaged to another woman, and Donna is still angry about it. She sings **"The Winner Takes It All"** remembering the old predicament and her feelings. It's never clear who Sophie's father really is, but she comes to love all three men. She calls her wedding off, but Donna connects with her old beau Sam, who is now single and available. The wedding plans stay in place, but Donna and Sam get married instead. The show is a good time for audiences familiar with the great pop songs of the score.

ON A CLEAR DAY YOU CAN SEE FOREVER

MUSIC: Burton Lane
BOOK AND LYRICS: Alan Jay Lerner
DIRECTOR: Robert Lewis
CHOREOGRAPHER: Herbert Ross
OPENED: October 17, 1965, New York; a run of 280 performances

Alan Jay Lerner's fascination with the phenomenon of extrasensory perception led to his teaming with composer Richard Rodgers in 1962 to write a musical to be called *I Picked a Daisy*. When that didn't work out, Lerner turned to composer Burton Lane, with whom he'd worked in Hollywood years before. The result is a show about Daisy Gamble (Barbara Harris in the original cast), a flakey but lovable young New York free spirit who has an extraordinary talent for growing plants, can predict when the phone will ring, and has noticeable ESP abilities. To quit smoking she seeks out hypnosis with Dr. Mark Bruckner, but it emerges that while hypnotized she can recall her past life as Melinda Wells in 18th century London. Mark becomes infatuated with Melinda, who emerges as a romantic rival to the present-day Daisy, which infuriates Daisy. They split up, but he persuades her to come back. Daisy opens the show singing **"Hurry! It's Lovely Up Here!"** in the solarium of the Bruckner Clinic, coaxing plants to grow. Barbra Streisand starred in the 1970 Vincente Minnelli film adaptation of the musical.

THE PIRATE QUEEN

MUSIC: Claude-Michel Schönberg
LYRICS: Alain Boublil, Richard Maltby, Jr. and John Dempsey
BOOK: Alain Boublil, Claude-Michel Schönberg and Richard Maltby, Jr.
DIRECTOR: Frank Galati
CHOREOGRAPHER: Graciela Daniele
OPENED: April 5, 2007, New York; a run of 85 performances

The musical about a swashbuckling heroine of the seas is based on the novel *Grania—She King of the Irish Seas* by Morgan Llywelyn. Clan feuds dominate 16th century Ireland. At the christening of the new ship, *The Pirate Queen*, a Chieftain's daughter, 18-year-old Grace O'Malley (Grania), tells her father she wants to be a sailor. After hearing that such a dream is impossible and being ordered from the christening ceremony with the other women, Grace sings to her sweetheart, Tiernan, her frustration in **"Woman."** After disguising herself as a cabin boy her career at sea begins. When Grace proves herself in battle, her father trains her to be a sea captain. The complex story has her as a leader in making peace with other clans in Ireland, and in defying Queen Elizabeth I and the English.

RENT

MUSIC, LYRICS AND BOOK: Jonathan Larson
DIRECTOR: Michael Greif
CHOREOGRAPHER: Marls Yearby
OPENED: Off-Broadway on February 29, 1996, New York; Broadway on April 29, 1996

Jonathan Larson's musical relocates the story of Puccini's opera *La Bohème* to the 1990s in New York's East Village. Among other stories and characters, Roger Davis is an ex-junkie HIV-positive songwriter/musician whose past girlfriend, a drug addict, died of AIDS. He meets Mimi Marquez, a heroin addict, and there is an obvious spark of attraction between them. He is initially terrified of getting involved with her, but after he finds out that she is HIV-positive as well, they begin a romance. They live together for a time, but have a tempestuous relationship. Roger is extremely jealous and leaves her. Mimi contemplates being alone in **"Without You."** Months later friends bring a desperately ill Mimi back to Roger, and she dies. The compelling alternative-rock score has a gritty realism, a theatrical reflection of grunge rock of the period. A parable of hope, love and loyalty, *Rent* received great acclaim, winning the Pulitzer Prize for Drama, a Tony Award for Best Musical, and many other awards. Though it initially opened Off-Broadway in the New York Theatre Workshop, it soon transferred to a Broadway theatre that was redesigned to capture its East Village atmosphere. Bound up with the show's message of the preciousness of life is the tragic real-life story of its composer/librettist Jonathan Larson, who died suddenly of an aortic dissection the night of the final dress rehearsal before the first Off-Broadway preview performance. A 2005 film version featured most of the original Broadway cast.

SONG AND DANCE

MUSIC: Andrew Lloyd Webber
LYRICS: Don Black, Richard Maltby, Jr.
ADAPTATION: Richard Maltby, Jr.
DIRECTOR: Richard Maltby, Jr.
CHOREOGRAPHER: Peter Martins
OPENED: March 26, 1982, London; September 18, 1985, New York; a run of 474 performances

The "Dance" of the title originated in 1979 when Andrew Lloyd Webber composed a set of variations on Paganini's A minor Capriccio that seemed to him to be perfect for a ballet. The "Song" originated a year later with a one-woman British television musical, *Tell Me on a Sunday,* which consisted entirely of musical pieces. Two years after that, both works were presented together in London as a full evening's entertainment, now connected with a bit of plot. A revised version opened in New York, winning high praise for Bernadette Peters, whose task in Act I was to create, without dialogue or other actors, the character of a free-spirited English young woman, Emma, who has relationships of varying sorts with four American men. **"Take That Look Off Your Face"** opens the show and the audience gets a first impression of Emma, freshly arrived from London. She has dreamed of being in New York and is addressing Viv (though there is no actor on stage playing Viv), an old friend from England who has been in New York for a year.

SOPHISTICATED LADIES

MUSIC: Duke Ellington
LYRICS: Various writers
DIRECTOR: Michael Smuin
CONCEPT: Donald McKayle
CHOREOGRAPHY: Donald McKayle and Michael Smuin
OPENED: March 1, 1981, New York; a run of 767 performances

Though different in concept, *Sophisticated Ladies* followed the lead of *Ain't Misbehavin'* and *Eubie!* in previous years by being a plotless revue entertainment built around the catalogue of a single composer. This celebration of the music of Duke Ellington was conceived as an elaborate, brassy nightclub floor show, with a 21-piece on-stage orchestra, led by Ellington's son Mercer Ellington, and a cast of 17, with first rate dancers (Gregory Hines, Judith Jamison) and singers. Its opening night of the tryout run in Washington had gone so badly that director Donald McKayle, who had conceived the production, was replaced by ballet choreographer Michael Smuin. Despite his inexperience in the world of Broadway, Smuin turned things around by adding nine songs, rearranging the sequence of the 36 numbers, introducing new dances, and dropping all existing dialogue.

MONTY PYTHON'S SPAMALOT

MUSIC: John Du Prez and Eric Idle
LYRICS AND BOOK: Eric Idle
DIRECTOR: Mike Nichols
CHOREOGRAPHER: Casey Nicholaw
OPENED: March 17, 2005, New York

Eric Idle, one of the founding members of the British television comedy troupe "Monty Python's Flying Circus," made his Broadway writing debut with Monty Python's Spamalot, billed as "a new musical lovingly ripped off from the motion picture Monty Python and the Holy Grail." As in the movie, the show involves the wacky adventures of King Arthur and his band of knights in their search for the Holy Grail, shrubbery, and in the musical, success on the Great White Way. The lavish *Spamalot* was directed by luminary Broadway and movie director Mike Nichols. The original cast starred Tim Curry, Hank Azaria and David Hyde Pierce. True to characteristic Python irreverence and silliness, *Spamalot* lambasts the musical genre at every step. The Lady of the Lake (Sara Ramirez won a Tony Award for the role) mocks the overly earnest, over-decorated style of a pop diva in "Find Your Grail." *Spamalot* won the 2005 Tony Award for Best Musical.

SPRING AWAKENING

MUSIC: Duncan Sheik
LYRICS AND BOOK: Steven Sater
DIRECTOR: Michael Mayer
CHOREOGRAPHER: Bill T. Jones
OPENED: December 10, 2006

This rock musical, 2007 Tony Award winner of Best Musical, is based on the 1891 German play by Frank Wedekind, which was banned for decades because of its frankness about teenage sex and suicide. The setting is a provincial German town in the 1890s. Teenagers struggle against strict morals of adults and the lack of instruction and communication about sex and emotion. Wendla Bergmann is a girl discovering her sexuality and sensuality in a time that forbids such things. She opens the show singing **"Mama Who Bore Me"** about all her mother has not told her. In **"The Dark I Know Well"** the adolescent Martha confides to friends that her father sexually abuses her and that her mother refuses to do anything about it. Martha asks her friends to not tell anyone else, so that she does not end up like Ilse, a friend from childhood who now wanders homeless and aimless because her parents kicked her out of their house. The song is sung by Martha and Ilse, adapted as a solo in this edition.

SWEET CHARITY

MUSIC: Cy Coleman
LYRICS: Dorothy Fields
BOOK: Neil Simon
DIRECTOR/CHOREOGRAPHER: Bob Fosse
OPENED: Janury 29, 1966, New York; a run of 608 performances

Bob Fosse initiated the project, based on the Federico Fellini 1957 film *Le Notti di Cabiria*. Originally intended as the first half of a double bill of one-act musicals, *Sweet Charity* was fleshed out to two acts when Neil Simon took over the writing. Charity Hope Valentine (originally played by Gwen Verdon) is a New York dance hall hostess who knows there's gotta be something better than working at the Fandango Ballroom. She is big-hearted and open to anything that comes her way. As she walks past the Pompeii Club an Italian movie star, Vittorio Vidal, comes out while chasing his mistress, who has stormed out. When she refuses to return to the club with him, he instead invites Charity, who just happens to be there. She accepts, but faints due to hunger while dancing with him. He takes her back to his apartment. Charity suddenly feels fine once there and can't believe her luck at being in such luxurious surroundings in the home of a celebrity, singing **"If My Friends Could See Me Now."** She later gets seriously involved with straight-laced, neurotic tax accountant Oscar Lindquist after they meet while stuck in an elevator. Afraid of what Oscar will think of her, Charity keeps her profession a secret. At one point she has had enough and quits the Fandango Ballroom, wandering in Times Square, wondering **"Where Am I Going?"** She works up the nerve to tell Oscar the truth, and finds out he already knows since he followed her one night. He says it doesn't matter and asks Charity to marry him. She is thrilled, but eventually Oscar calls off the engagement, saying he can't get Charity's history with other men out of his mind. The play ends with, "And so she lived... *hopefully*... ever after." *Sweet Charity* has been revived twice to date on Broadway, in 1986 and 2007. A film version, directed by Bob Fosse and starring Shirley MacLaine, was released in 1969. John McMartin repeated his stage role as Oscar in the movie.

TARZAN

MUSIC AND LYRICS: Phil Collins
BOOK: David Henry Hwang
DIRECTOR: Bob Crowley
CHOREOGRAPHER: Meryl Tankard
OPENED: May 10, 2006, New York; a run of 486 performances

Tarzan the stage musical is faithfully based on the 1999 Disney animated film *Tarzan,* (screenplay by Tab Murphy, Bob Tzudiker and Noni White), which was based on the adventure novel *Tarzan of the Apes* by Edgar Rice Burroughs. Phil Collins sang all the songs in the film. These were adapted for characters in the story to sing in the stage version, and Collins also added new songs. The setting is the west coast of Africa, 1888. A mother gorilla, Kala, discovers a human infant whose parents have been killed. Against her mate's strong objections, she vows to keep the baby and raise him as her own offspring, singing **"You'll Be in My Heart"** to the tiny child.

THOROUGHLY MODERN MILLIE

MUSIC: Jeanine Tesori
LYRICS: Dick Scanlan
BOOK: Dick Scanlan and Richard Morris
DIRECTOR: Michael Mayer
CHOREOGRAPHER: Rob Ashford
OPENED: April 18, 2002, New York; a run of 903 performances

Based on the 1967 movie starring Julie Andrews, *Thoroughly Modern Millie* the stage musical retains only three songs from the film (including the title song), with a score of principally new material. The story chronicles the life of Millie (Sutton Foster won a Tony for the part in the original cast), a small-town Kansas girl in New York of 1922. She is anxious and afraid but excited to be in the big city, and definitely decides to stay there, and not return home, singing **"Not for the Life of Me."** Millie stays with other young starlets at the Hotel Priscilla, which is run by the sinister Mrs. Meers, who actually is running a white slave trade on the side. Millie gets a job as a stenographer at the Sincere Trust Insurance Company. She intends to marry her wealthy boss, but falls for a charming but poor paper clip salesman, Jimmy Smith. The madcap plot has many twists and turns, and shows a cheery slice of flapper life in New York during the Jazz age. Millie decides in the end that it is only love she is interested in, and agrees to marry Jimmy.

TICK, TICK...BOOM!

MUSIC, LYRICS AND BOOK: Jonathan Larson
DIRECTOR: Scott Schwartz
CHOREOGRAPHER: Christopher Gattelli
OPENED: May 23, 2001, New York, closed 1/6/02

Jonathan Larson, composer of *Rent*, struggled like many actors and writers in New York for years before he found success. After the unproduced *Superbia*, tick...tick...BOOM! was his second musical. Initially it was a one-man show that told Larson's autobiographical story about bohemian life in New York, which he performed himself at various times between 1989 and 1993. He lives on virtually nothing, passing up lucrative corporate job offers to follow his dream. Larson shelved it to spend time on *Rent*. After his death, interest in his earlier work emerged, and in 2001, *tick...tick...BOOM!* received a full Off-Broadway production, expanded to a three-character piece: Jonathan, his girlfriend Susan, and his best friend Michael. The show opens on a Saturday night in 1990, with Jonathan soon turning 30. Jonathan's musical is in workshop, *Superbia*, and an actress in the show (the actor who plays Susan also plays this character) sings **"Come to Your Senses,"** which is actually from Larson's unproduced show *Superbia*. After Michael reveals that he is HIV-positive, Jonathan contemplates their long friendship and the importance of every day as he faces his 30th birthday.

WICKED

MUSIC AND LYRICS: Stephen Schwartz
BOOK: Winnie Holzman, based on the novel *Wicked: The Life and Times of the Wicked Witch of the West* by Gregory Maguire
DIRECTOR: Joe Mantello
CHOREOGRAPHER: Wayne Cilento
OPENED: October 30, 2003, New York

Stephen Schwartz's return to Broadway came with the hit musical *Wicked*. Based on Gregory Maguire's 1995 book, the musical chronicles the backstory of the Elphaba, the "Wicked Witch of the West," and Glinda (actually name Galinda), the "Good Witch of the North," before their story threads are picked up in L. Frank Baum's *The Wonderful Wizard of Oz*. In Emerald City the Wizard tricks Elphaba into using the Grimmerie (an ancient book of witch spells) to give Chistery, his monkey servant, the ability to fly, After she realizes that she has been used by the duplicitous Wizard, Elphaba runs off with the Grimmerie, being chased by the Wizard's palace guards. After being labeled "wicked" Elphaba casts a spell on a broomstick to make it fly, and she flies off, vowing to fight the Wizard in the song **"Defying Gravity,"** which ends Act I. After Elphaba captures Dorothy, Glinda tries to persuade Elphaba to release her, but Elphaba refuses. She makes Glinda promise not to clear her hame and to take control of Oz from the Wizard. Glinda and Elphaba sing of real friendship in **"For Good."** Though it appears that she was melted by water, Elphaba escapes through a trap door and escapes with Fiyero. The original cast included Kristin Chenoweth as Glinda, Idina Menzel as Elphaba, Norbert Leo Butz as Fiyero, and Joel Grey as the Wizard.

WORKING

MUSIC AND LYRICS: Stephen Schwartz, Craig Carnelia, James Taylor, Micki Grant, Mary Rodgers and Susan Birkenhead
BOOK AND DIRECTION: Stephen Schwartz
CHOREOGRAPHER: Onna White
OPENED: May 14, 1978, New York; a run of 25 performances

Adapted from Studs Terkel's Pulitzer-winning book of interviews with all walks of working men and women, this revue-type musical follows a typical work day around the clock. We meet a waitress, a fireman, a builder, a teacher, a retiree, a cleaning lady, a parking lot attendant, a millworker, and many more, offering a cross-section of attitudes about the kind of work people do and why they do it. Some of their stories are funny, some stoic, some deeply touching. As Terkel put it, "Its theme is about a search for daily meaning as well as daily bread, for recognition as well as cash." To express its eclectic characters, *Working* has a score made up of songs by an assortment of writers with a variety of distinctive styles and ethnic backgrounds. As dinnertime sets in at a restaurant, Delores, a waitress, turns her job of serving food into a one-woman show in the song **"It's an Art."**

ZORBA

MUSIC: John Kander
LYRICS: Fred Ebb
BOOK: Joseph Stein, adapted from *Zorba the Greek* by Nikos Kazantzakis
DIRECTOR: Harold Prince
CHOREOGRAPHER: Ronald Field
OPENED: November 16, 1968, New York; a run of 305

The musical was adapted from Nikos Kazantzakis' 1952 novel *Zorba the Greek* and the 1964 film of the same name. On the island of Crete the larger-than-life Zorba, an aging hero of the story, meets a young American man, Nikos, who has inherited an abandoned, inoperable mine on the island. The musical tells of a series of tragic, related events: the suicide of a young Cretan man out of unrequited love for a young widow, the vengeful murder of the widow by the dead youth's family, and the death of Hortense, a woman in love with Zorba. Nothing, however, can dampen Zorba's lust for life. At the top of the show a character simply named Leader, one of the Cretan women, tells of their philosophy in **"Life Is."** Anthony Quinn, who starred in the 1964 movie, starred in a 1983 Broadway revival.

CITY LIGHTS
from *The Act*

Words by FRED EBB
Music by JOHN KANDER

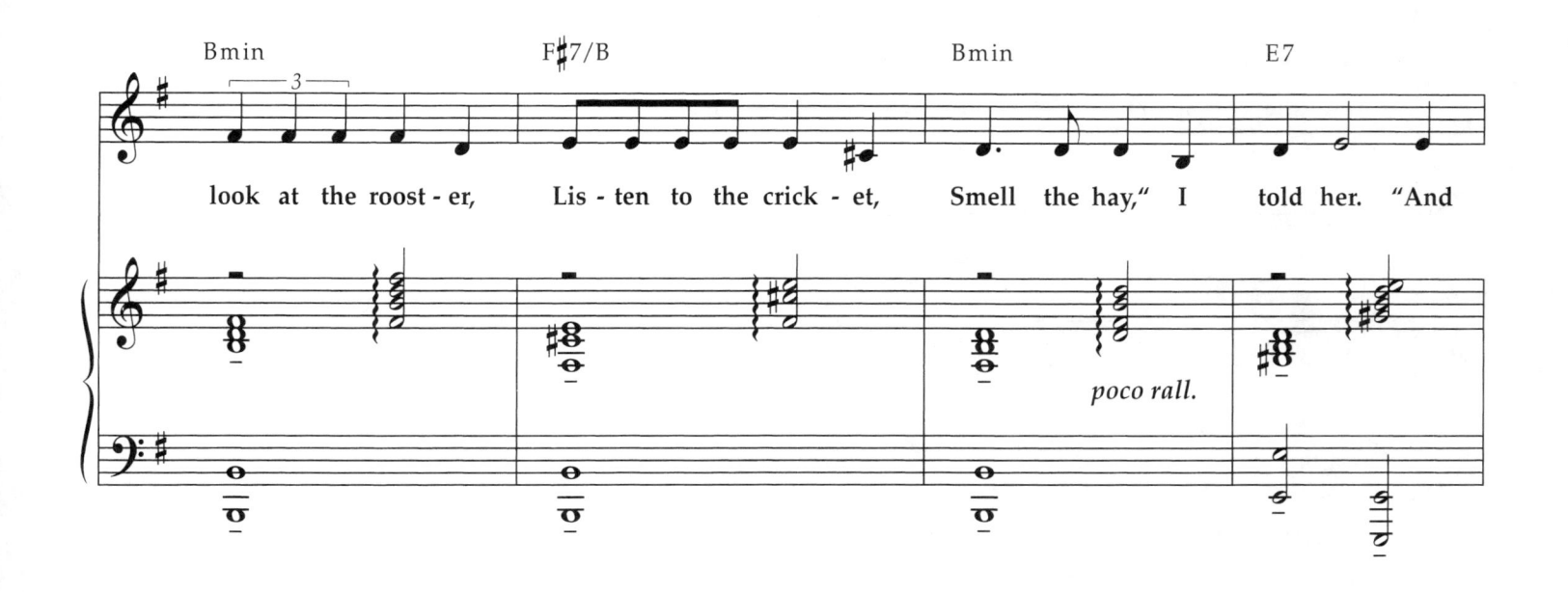

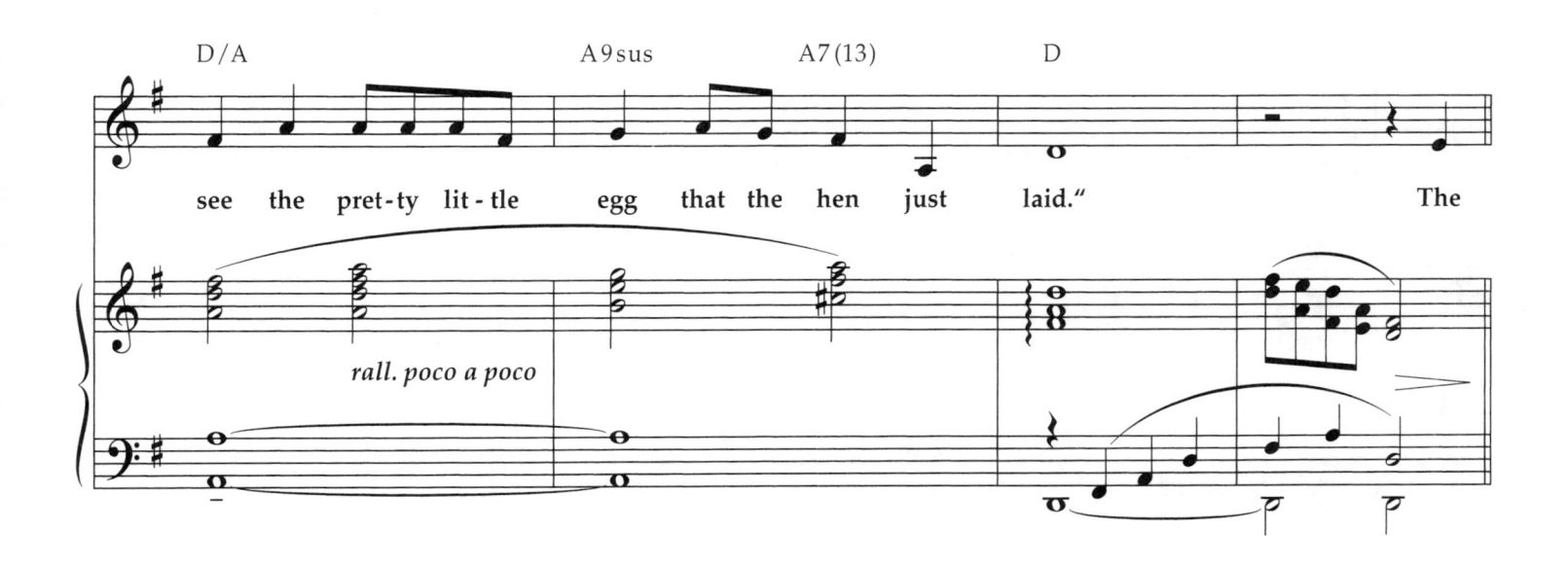

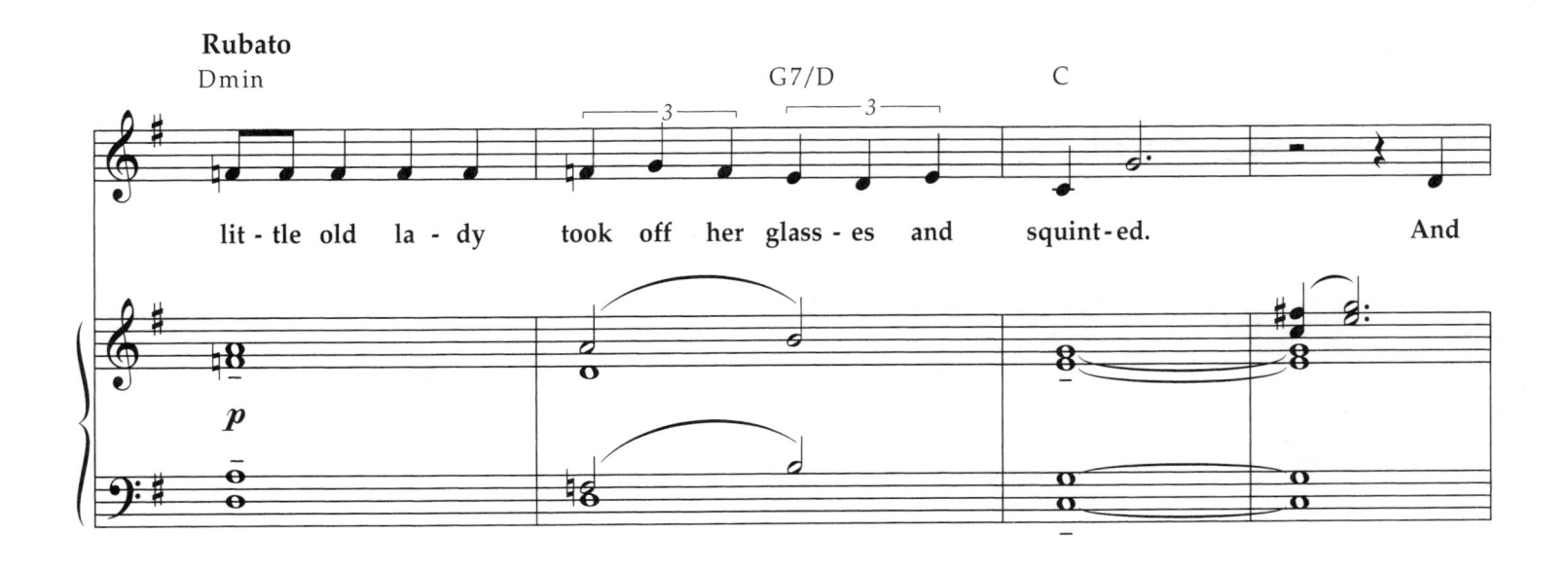

look at the roost-er, Lis-ten to the crick-et, Smell the hay," I told her. "And see the pret-ty lit-tle egg that the hen just laid." The

Rubato

lit-tle old la-dy took off her glass-es and squint-ed. And

how she re-spond-ed lit-er-al-ly had me floored. *She said: "I'm glad to meet some-one who ap - pre - ci - ates The beau-ty that na-ture in - i - ti - ates. It's sweet to hear, But me, my dear, I'm tru - ly bored.* I miss those

Medium slow Rag
G
G(6)
Gmaj7
cit - y lights
Those spark - a - ling
cit - y lights,
marc.
sim.
G7
Cmaj7
C♯dim7
3
Those twink - a - ling
cit - y lights
blur - ring my
Bmin
F♯/A♯
Amin
D7
G
eyes.
I love those
cit - y lights,
marc.
G(6)
Gmaj7
G7
The col - or of
cit - y sights
That shine un - der

Cmaj7
C♯dim7
B
F♯7sus
B
city lights
tint-ing the skies.
cresc.
C
Cmin
G/B
New - mown hay gives me hay fe - ver. There's the roost - er,
mf
Emin
A7
where's my cleav - er? So laid back, my mind might crack. And
Cmin(6)/E♭
D9(13)
when the thresh - er's up,
My pres - sure's up.

G
G(6)
Gmaj7
Cit - y lights, I long for those cit - y lights,
marc.
sim.
G7
Cmaj7
C
B7
Those beau - ti - ful cit - y lights beck - on - ing
Emin(9)
D7
G7
C
Cmin
me there. Be there. Take the crick - ets and go shove 'em,
cresc.
f
G/B
A7
Amin7
Ur - ban cri - ses, how I love 'em! Grime and grit and

pret - ty cit - y lights.

Walk - ing lanes to pick a dai - sy, That can tru - ly drive you cra - zy. Home - made bread lies here like lead. And Pol - ly's peach pre - serves, Oh, please, my nerves!

City lights, ___ I long ___ for those city lights. ___
The bulbs ___ of those beaming brights ___ beckoning
me there. ___ Be there. ___ Sties and stables sure are smelly,
Let me sniff some kosher deli. Brightly lit by

pret - ty cit - y lights.

Pluck your lil - ies of the val - ley, Let me sal - ly up some al - ley Dim - ly lit by pret - ty cit - y lights.

Pull back

Country air means "zilch" to me, I won't breathe nothin' I can't see. So, lemme quit and hit those city lights. Love those city city lights."

KEEPIN' OUT OF MISCHIEF NOW

featured in *Ain't Misbehavin'*

Lyric by ANDY RAZAF
Music by THOMAS "FATS" WALLER

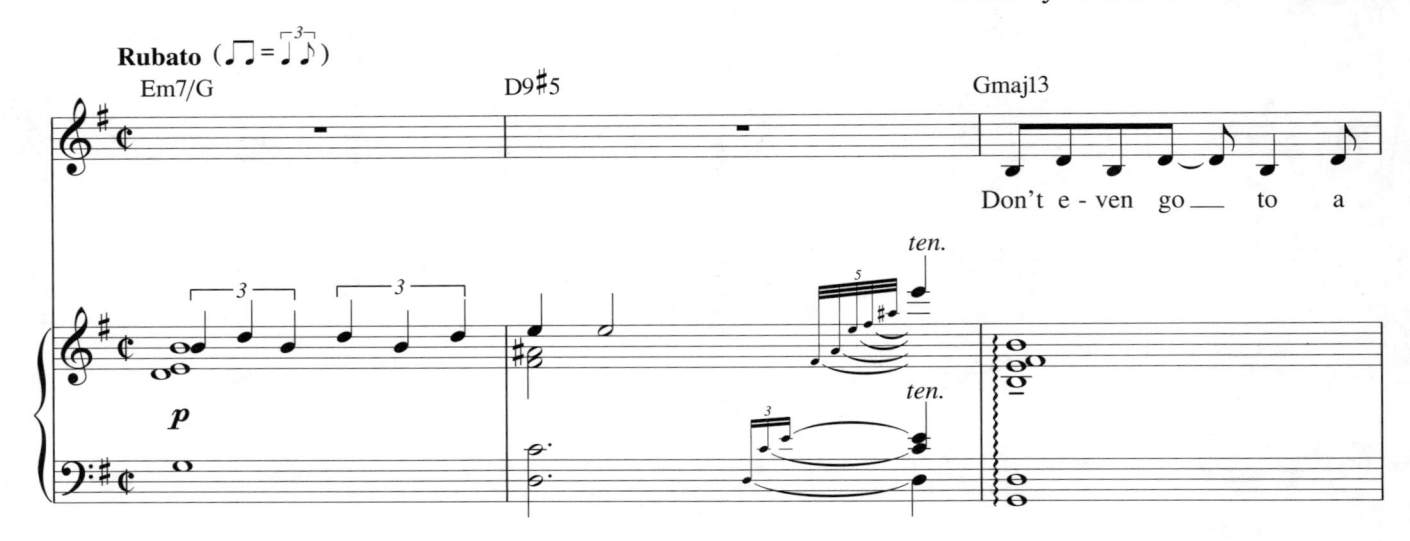

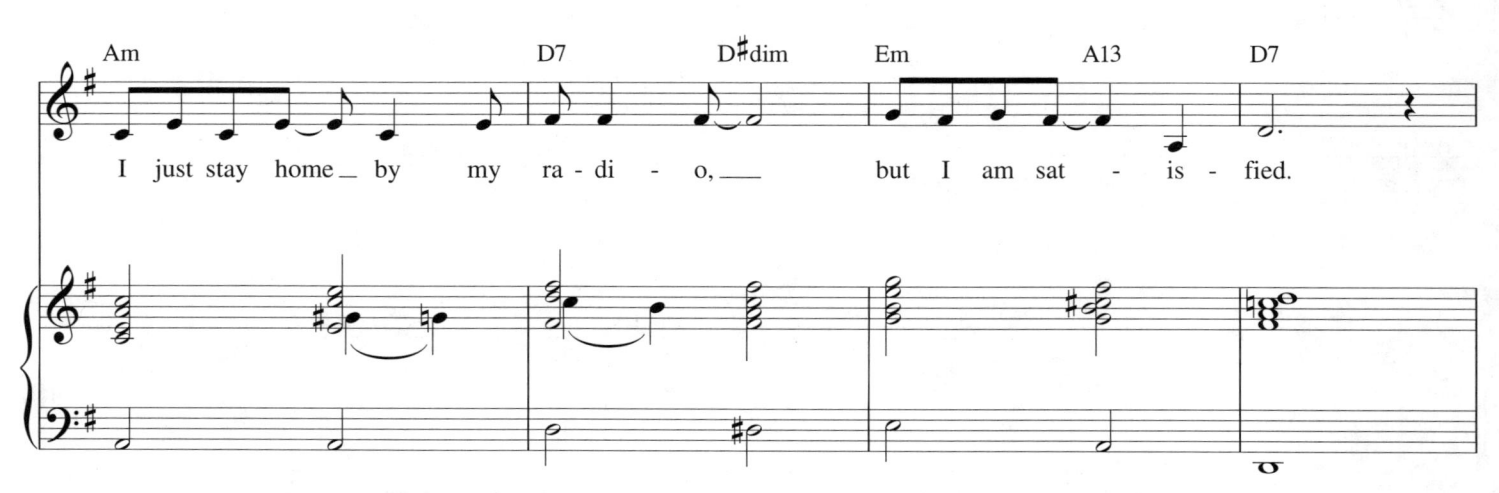

Don't e - ven go to a mov - ie show, if you are not at my side. I just stay home by my ra - di - o, but I am sat - is - fied.

© 1932 EDWIN H. MORRIS & COMPANY, A Division of MPL Music Publishing, Inc.
© Renewed 1960 EDWIN H. MORRIS & COMPANY, A Division of MPL Music Publishing, Inc. and CHAPPELL & CO.
All Rights Reserved

All my flirt-ing days are gone, on the lev-el from now on.

Moderately Slow Ballad

Keep-in' out of mis-chief now, real-ly am in love and how.

I'm through play-in' with fire, it's you whom I de-sire. All the world can plain-ly see, you're the on-ly one for me. I have told them in ad-vance, they can't break up our ro-mance. Liv-in' up to ev-'ry vow, keep-in' out of mis-chief now. Don't go for an-y ex-cite-ment now. Books are my best com-pa-

F7 Gm7♭5 A♭m6 F7 B♭m E♭7 Edim
ny. All my op - in - ions have changed some - how,
Rubato
Fm B♭13 E♭7 B♭m7 E♭9 B♭m7 E♭9
old fash - ioned as can be. When you real - ly
ritard.
p
E♭m6 F7 B♭9 E♭7 Adim
learn to care, there's a thrill in sol - i - taire.
accel. e cresc.
Tempo I
B♭m9 E♭13 B♭m9 E♭13 A♭6 E♭13
All the world can plain - ly see, you're the on - ly one for
mp

28

SPECIAL
from the Broadway Musical *Avenue Q*

Music and Lyrics by ROBERT LOPEZ
and JEFF MARX

Sexy Jazz (♪♪ = ♪♪³) *(medium slow)*

LUCY THE SLUT:
I can make you feel spe - cial ___ when it sucks to be you. Let me make you feel spe - cial ___ for an hour ___ or two. ___ Your

Copyright © 2003 Only For Now, Inc. and Fantasies Come True, Inc. (administered by R&H Music)
International Copyright Secured   All Rights Reserved
For more info about Avenue Q, visit www.AvenueQ.com

Avenue Q has not been authorized or approved in any manner by The Jim Henson Company or Sesame Workshop which have no responsibility for its content.

*Possible cut to ** for auditions.

(spoken:) *Yeah, they're real.*

When we're to-geth-er, the earth will shake, and the stars will fall in-to the sea. So come on, ba-by, let down your guard. When your date's in the bath-room, I'll slip you my card. I can tell just by look-ing that you've got it hard for

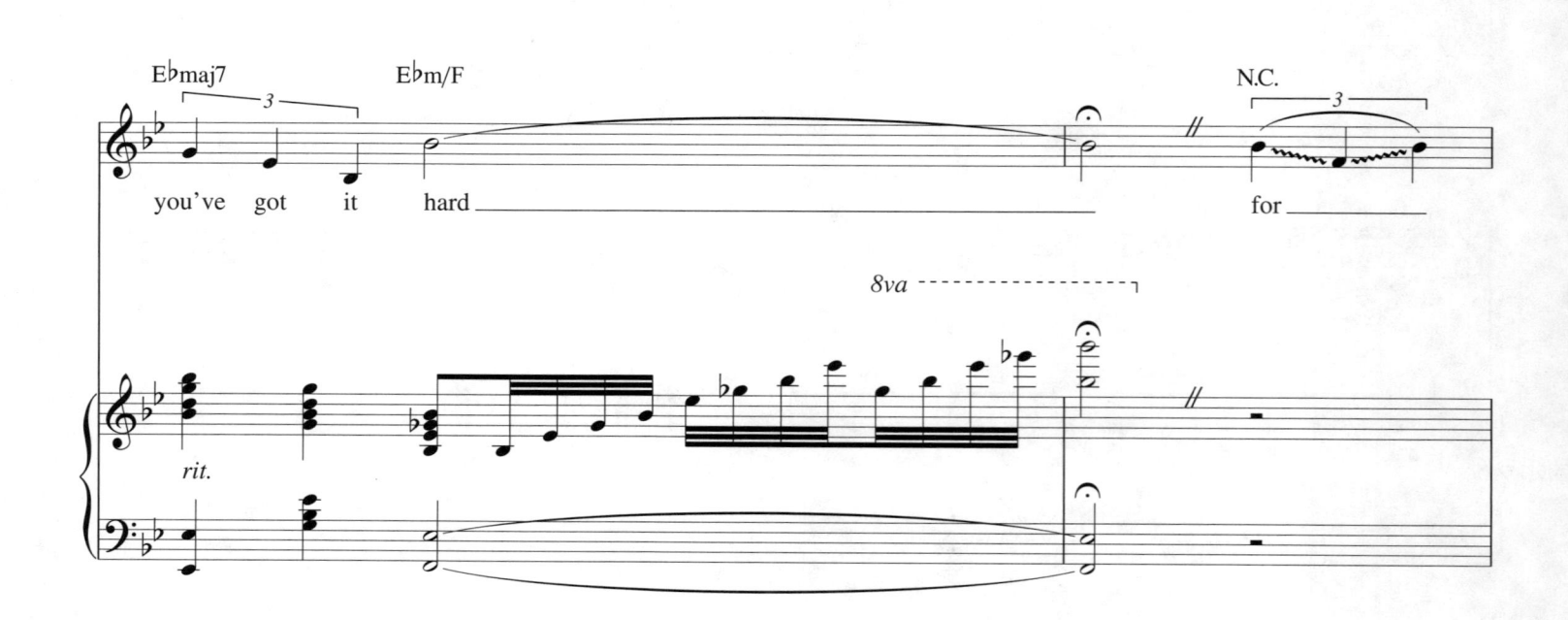

33

MEADOWLARK
from *The Baker's Wife*

Music and Lyrics by
STEPHEN SCHWARTZ

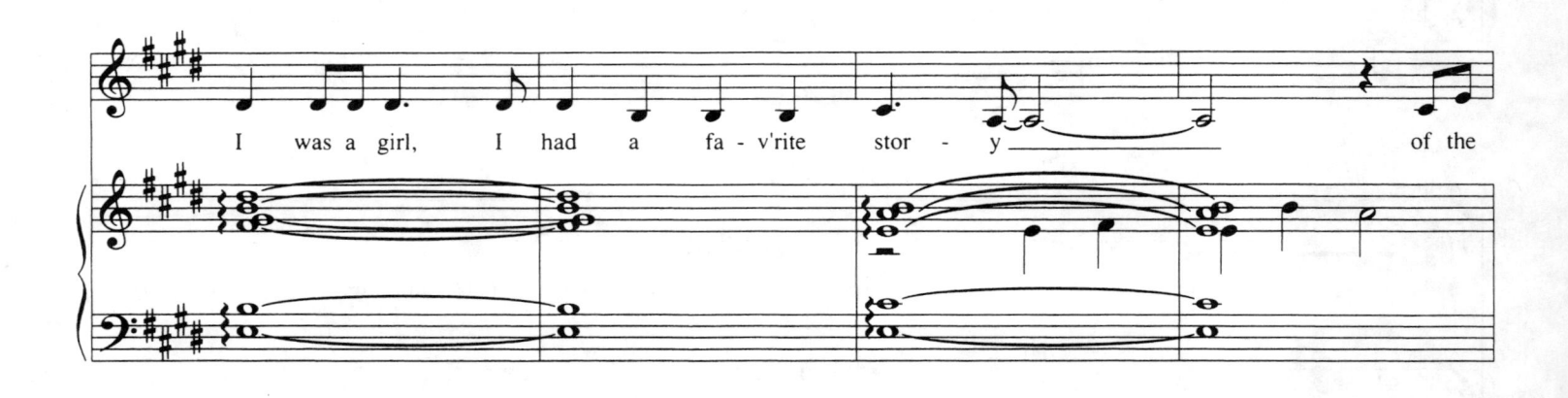

GENEVIEVE:

When I was a girl, I had a fav'rite story of the meadowlark who lived where the rivers wind. Her

Light, child like

sfp *p*

Copyright © 1976 Grey Dog Music
Copyright Renewed
Publishing and allied rights for "Meadowlark" administered by Williamson Music
International Copyright Secured   All Rights Reserved
www.stephenschwartz.com

voice could match the an - gels' in its glor - y, but she was blind, the lark was blind. An old king came and took her to his pal - ace where the walls were bur - nished bronze and gol - den braid. And he fed her fruit and nuts from an iv-'ry cha-lice and he prayed: "Sing for

accelerando poco a poco

1. me my mea-dow-lark, sing for me of the sil-ver
2. me my mea-dow-lark, fly with me on the sil-ver

mor - ning. Set me free, _____
mor - ning. Past the sea _____

_____ my mea - dow - lark _____ and I'll
_____ where the dol - phins bark _____ we will

buy you a price - less jew - el, _____ and cloth of bro - cade and
dance on the cor - al bea - ches, _____ make a feast of the plums and

crew - el, _____ and I'll love you for life if you will _____
pea - ches, _____ just as far as your vi - sion rea - ches _____

sing for me."
fly with me."

Then one day as the lark sang by the wa-ter, the God of the sun heard her in his flight

and her sing-ing moved him so he came and brought her ___ the gift ___ of sight. ___ He gave ___ her sight ___ and she o-pened her eyes ___ to the shim-mer ___ and the splen - dor ___ of this beau-ti-ful young God, so proud and strong. And he called to the lark in a voice both rough and ten-der. "Come a-long. Fly with

D. S. 𝄋 al Coda ⊕

8va bassa

Coda

But the mea-dow-lark said no, for the old king loved her so, she could-n't bear to wound his pride. So the Sun-God flew a-way, and when the king came down that day, he found his mea-dow-lark had died. Ev-'ry time I heard that part I cried. And

1. now I stand here star-ry eyed and stor-my oh, just when I thought my heart was fin-'lly numb, a beau-ti-ful young man ap-pears be-fore me, sing-ing:

2. what can I do if fin'-lly for the first time the one I'm bur-ning for re-turns the glow? If love has come at last, it's picked the worst time, still I

1.
"Come, oh, won't you come?"
And
2.
know
I've got to go! Fly a - way,
8va bassa
Gliss
8va bassa
mea - dow - lark, fly a -
3

way _____ in the sil-ver morn-ing. ____

If __ I __ stay, ____ I'll grow to curse the dark. ____ So it's off where the days won't bind me, ___ I know I leave wounds __ be-hind me but I

46

won't let to-mor-row find me _____ back _____ this way _____ be-fore my past once a-gain can blind me. Fly a-way.

And we won't __ wait to say good-bye, __ my beau-ti-ful young man __ and I.

col 8va bassa
rallentando *tempo*
rallentando *accelerando poco a poco*
8va bassa
rallentando *poco a poco accel*
8va bassa *8va bassa*

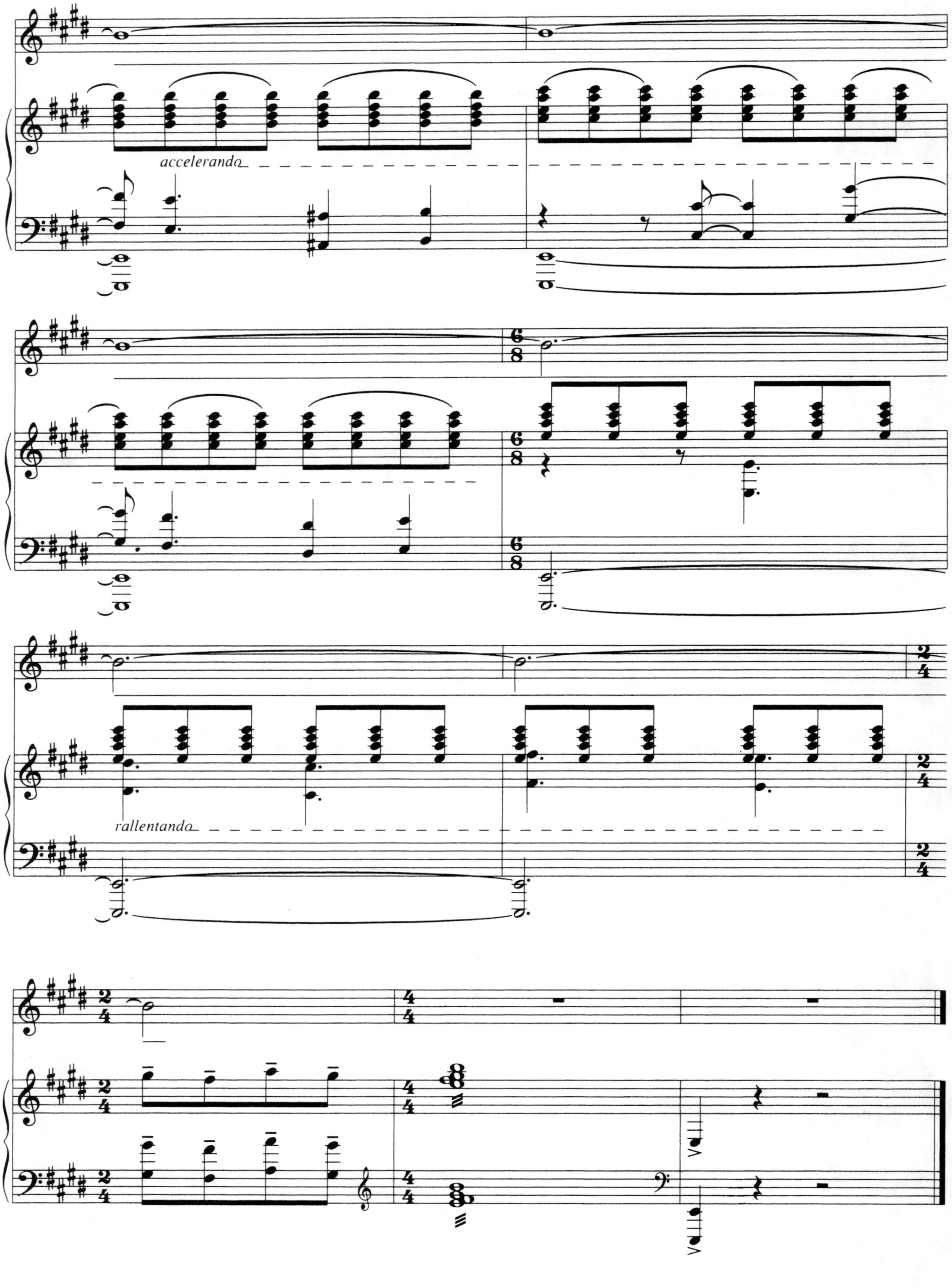
accelerando
rallentando

THE COLORS OF MY LIFE
from *Barnum*

Music by CY COLEMAN
Lyrics by MICHAEL STEWART

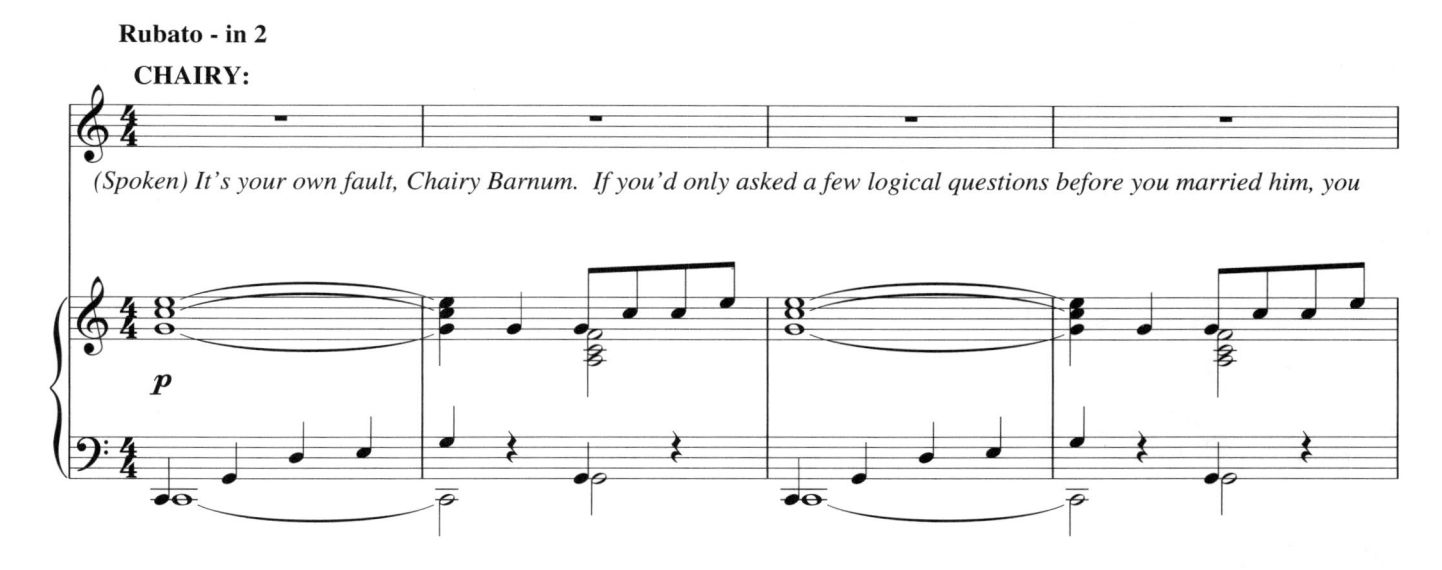

Rubato - in 2

CHAIRY:

(Spoken) It's your own fault, Chairy Barnum. If you'd only asked a few logical questions before you married him, you would've put a healthy distance between yourself and a fella who wants to give the whole world a paint job. Which I'm not so sure it needs!

The col-ors of my

A tempo - in 4

life ____ are soft-er than a breeze ____ the sil-ver grey of

Copyright © 1980 Notable Music Company, Inc.
All Rights Administered by Chrysalis Music
All Rights Reserved   Used by Permission

ei-der-down the dap-pled green of trees. The am-ber of a wheat-field the ha-zel of a seed, the crys-tal of a rain-drop are all I'll ev-er need. Your reds are much too bold, in gold I find no worth. I'll fill my days with sage and brown, the col-ors of the earth. And if from by my side my love should roam, the col-ors of my life will shine a qui-et light to lead him home.

IT'S A PERFECT RELATIONSHIP
from *Bells Are Ringing*

Words by BETTY COMDEN and ADOLPH GREEN
Music by JULE STYNE

Ad lib. (In 2)

ELLA: It's cra-zy, ri-dic-u-lous, it does-n't make sense. That's true, but what can I do?

Moderately fast

I'm in love with a

Copyright © 1956 by Betty Comden, Adolph Green and Jule Styne
Copyright Renewed
Stratford Music Corporation, owner of publication and allied rights throughout the world
Chappell & Co., administrator
International Copyright Secured All Rights Reserved

man, Plaza oh, double four, double three.

It's a perfect relationship. I can't see him, he can't see me. I'm in love with a voice, Plaza oh, double four, double three. What a perfect re-la-tion-ship. I talk to him, and he just talks to me. And yet I can't help won-d'ring what does he look like? I wish I knew.

What does he look like? Is he six foot seven or three foot two? Has he eyes of brown or baby blue? Big and mighty or under-fed? Trim black mustache or beard of red? — Can he dance like Fred As-taire? Is he dark or is he fair? He could be the fat and bald-ing type, — or rug-ged tweeds and a bri-ar pipe, — dark-rimmed glass-es, sup-er mind, — or the sweet po-et-

-ic kind.___ It does-n't mat-ter what he'd be,___ how he'd love me!

(Spoken) Susanswerphone. *Yes, Mr. Moss.* *Yes, Mr. Moss.* But he's still just a voice, Pla-za oh, dou-ble four, dou-ble three. What a per-fect re-

la - tion-ship. I can't see him, he can't see me. He calls me "mom," he thinks I'm six-ty three. And I'll nev-er meet him and he'll nev-er meet me. No, he'll nev-er meet me.

Bright tempo

WHAT YOU DON'T KNOW ABOUT WOMEN
from *City of Angels*

Music by CY COLEMAN
Lyrics by DAVID ZIPPEL

This is a duet for Gabby and Oolie adapted here as a solo.

Copyright © 1990 Notable Music Company, Inc.
All Rights Administered by Chrysalis Music
All Rights Reserved   Used by Permission

un - der - stand - ing lov - ers,_____ but nev - er un - der - stands the girl___ who lies be - neath the cov - ers._____ You on - ly have to o - pen up your mouth to show___ what you don't know___ and you don't know___ a - bout wom - en.___

A wom-an needs to be as-sured that she remains al-lur-ing; To now and then be re-as-sured your pas-sion is en-dur-ing. It's not e-nough to know your line to pol-ish and rou-tine it, and heav-en knows I know your line the whole rou-tine I've seen it, ya got-ta

62

mean it! What you don't know a-bout wom-en is what we need to hear. You think if you can sound sin-cere__ then we'll come run-nin' to__ you_____ throw in some truth for at-mos-phere,__ but we can see right through you. And ev-'ry hol-low com-pli-ment and phrase de-fines and un-der-lines what you don't know a-bout wom-en. You think what I don't know will not hurt me, but you don't know how of-ten you do.

How long a-go did good sense desert me? I don't know why I still burn for you. You're immature and short sighted, you're an incurable player, you show a lack of discretion, you don't know jack about heartache, you're out of sync with your feelings, you only

cresc. poco a poco

wink at com-mit-ment. You're run-ning low on e-mo - tion, what you don't know a-bout wom - en's on-ly a drop in the o - cean next to what you don't know _ a - bout me.

You are in need of a lit-tle en-light-'ning on la-dies and love but you can't see what you don't know a - bout wom - en is fright-'ning and you don't know noth-in' a - bout me.

CHILDREN OF EDEN
from *Children of Eden*

Music and Lyrics by
STEPHEN SCHWARTZ

Rubato

EVE: Like this brief day, my light is nearly gone.

But through the night, my children, you will go on.

You will know heartache, prayers that don't work. And

Copyright © 1991 Grey Dog Music (administered by Williamson Music)
International Copyright Secured All Rights Reserved

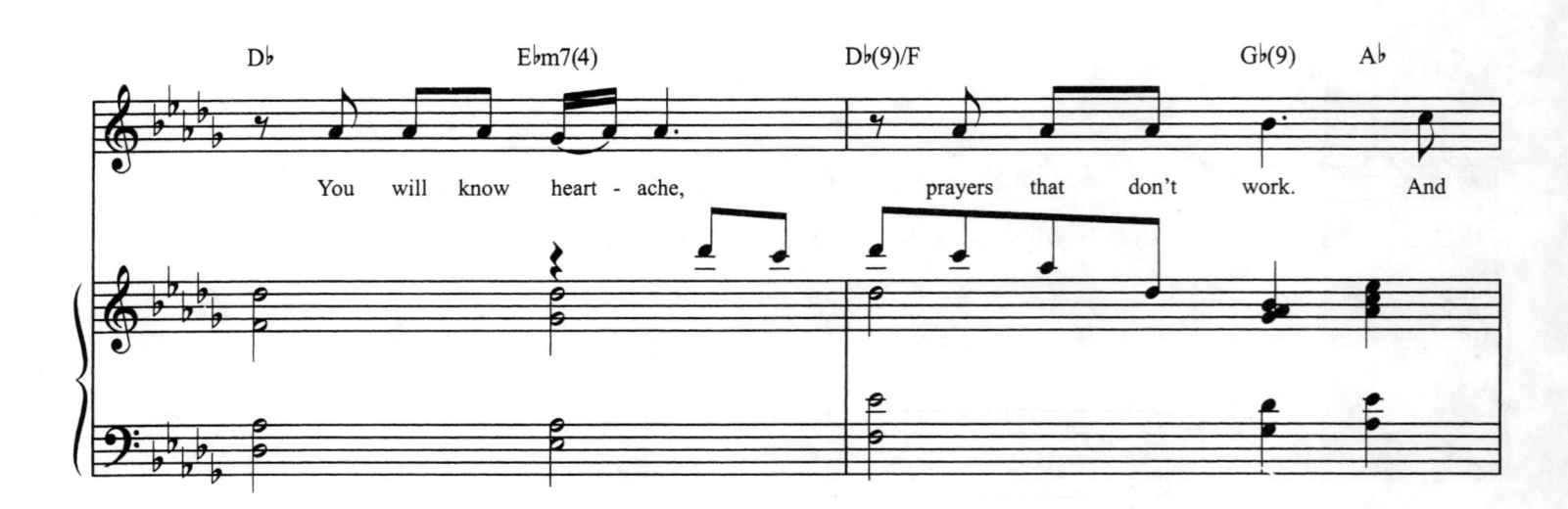

times of bit-ter cir-cum-stan-ces... But I still be-lieve in sec-ond chanc-es...

Gentle, flowing (♩=80)

Chil-dren of E-den, where have we left you?
Born to un-cer-tain-ty, des-tined for pain...

Sins of your parents haunt you and test you.

This, your inheritance: fire and rain.

Children of Eden, try not to blame us.

We were just human, to error prone.

D♭
E♭m7/D♭ D♭
E♭m G♭maj7 A♭
Chil - dren of E - den, will you re - claim__ us?
a tempo
Fm
B♭m
D♭/F
G♭6
Fm/A♭
You and your chil - dren to come, some - day
D/A
E/B
D♭
G♭(9)
to come home.
E D D♭sus/F D♭/G♭ D♭
p sub.

TOO BEAUTIFUL FOR WORDS
from the Broadway Musical *The Color Purple*

Words and Music by ALLEE WILLIS,
BRENDA RUSSELL and STEPHEN BRAY

Slowly and freely

SHUG:
Mm___ Mm___ I've al-ways been the kind of gal___ that had a lot to say.___ I says the things that's on my mind,___ too dumb to shy a-way.___ But you hush my mouth and still me___ with a song I nev-er heard.___ I

Copyright © 2004 Tonepet Music, Dimensional Songs Of The Knoll, Brenda Russell Music and Momma Hattie's Muse
Worldwide Rights for Dimensional Songs Of The Knoll and Brenda Russell Music Administered by Cherry River Music Co.
All Rights Reserved   Used by Permission

71

guess that means that you are just__ too beau-ti-ful for words. I

A tempo - Slow 4

seen this life from high and low, and all that's in-be-tween. I__

danced with dukes, crooned with counts, been court-ed like a queen.__ But__

when I see what's in your heart, all the past is blurred.__ The grace you bring in-to this world's too beau-ti-ful for words. You hide your head un-der your wings just like a lit-tle bird. Oh don't you know you're beau-ti-ful, too beau-ti-ful for words.

Oo, Ce-lie, you're too beau-ti-ful for words.
opt. Oo,

IT'S A BUSINESS
from *Curtains*

Music by JOHN KANDER
Lyrics by FRED EBB

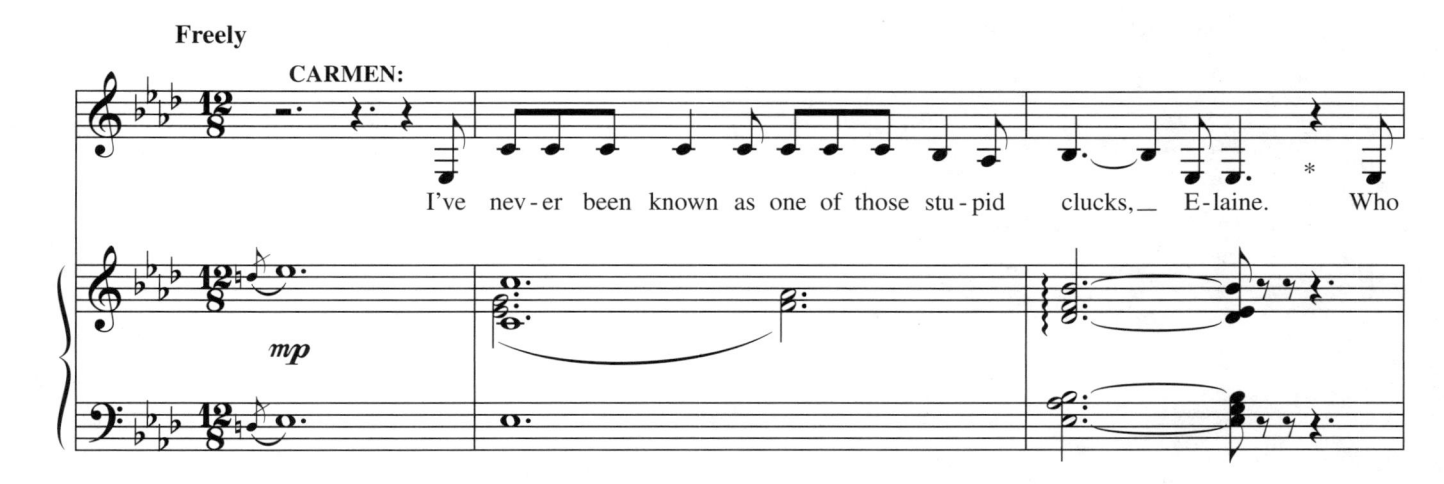

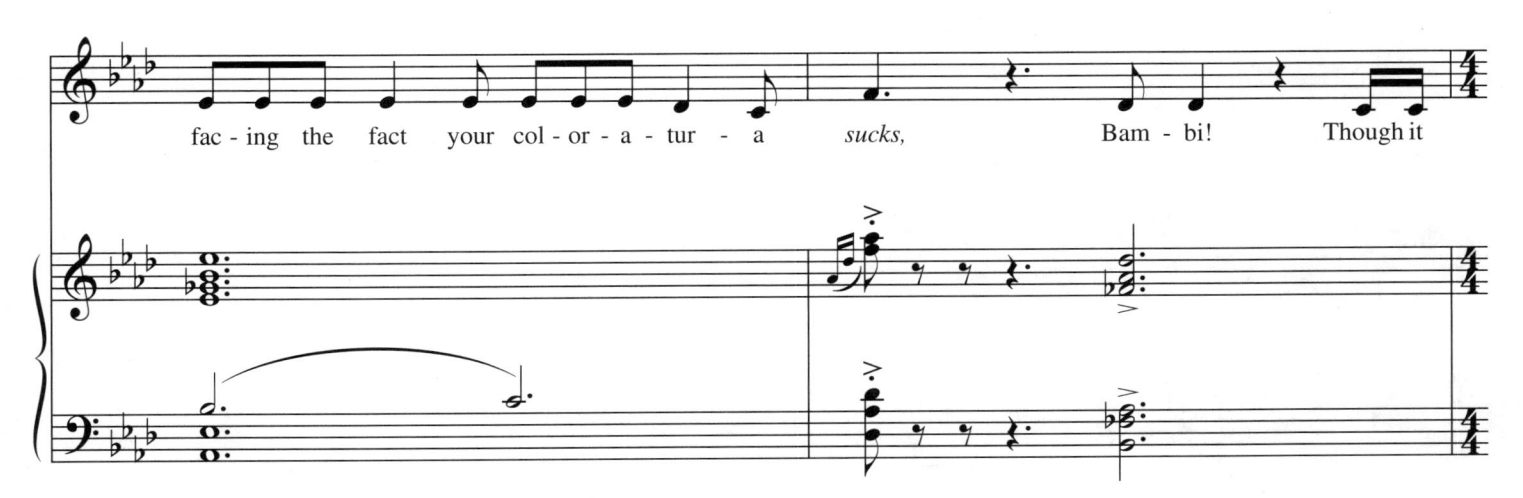

Freely

CARMEN: I've never been known as one of those stupid clucks, Elaine. Who pisses away a lot of her hard-earned bucks, Elaine. But facing the fact your coloratura *sucks*, Bambi! Though it

---

* In these two spots Carmen's daughter Elaine corrects her with her stage name, Bambi.
  Elaine is joined by ensemble in the show, eliminated in this solo edition.

Copyright © 2007 by Kander & Ebb, Inc.
All Rights Administered by Bro 'N Sis Music, Inc.
International Copyright Secured All Rights Reserved
Used by Permission

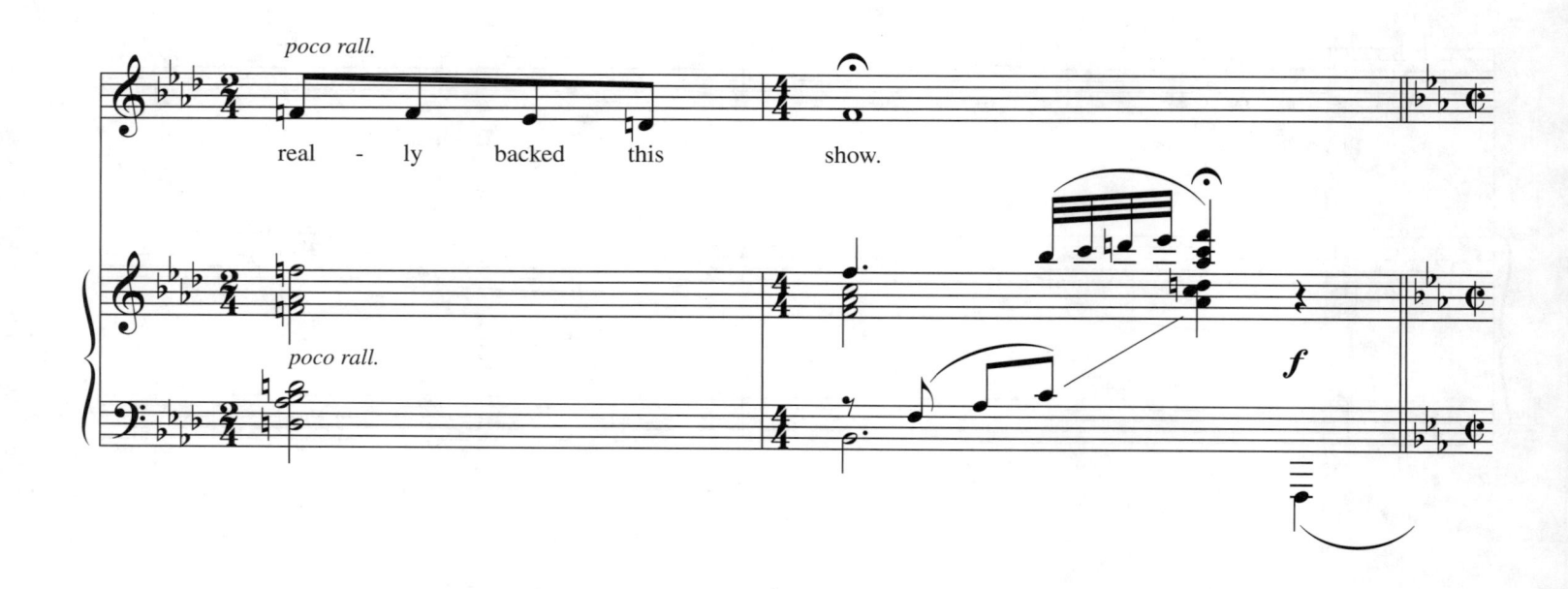

Con moto

breaks your moth-er's heart, For - get a - bout the part. It's time for you to know why I

colla voce

poco rall.

real - ly backed this show.

poco rall.

A Tempo - Coarse Strut

You

marc.

ask me for my motives well,__ you needn't be so smart.__ It's a
not-for-profit the-a-tre__ don't need to turn a buck.__ That's not

bus-'ness.
bus-'ness!
It
So,

is-n't mak-ing his-to-ry__ It is-n't mak-ing art,__ It's a
give them "Ly-sis-tra-ta" And__ I wish them lots of luck.__ I do

bus-'ness.
bus-'ness!

Shaw and Ibsen, Take 'em away. And don't bother me with Molière, Those Russian's never pay.

Gorky, Shmorky. money misspent. You won't survive Yom Kippur. You'll never get through Lent.

So, I go on, criticize me, Please proceed with your attack, It's a
I once knew a producer Whose pretention knew no bounds In the

bus - 'ness.
bus - 'ness.

I
He put one mil-lion in And I ex-pect two mil-ion back. It's a
mount-ed Sam-uel Beck-ett. I don't mean it like it sounds. It was

bus - 'ness.
bus - 'ness!

So what
So, crime have I com-mit-ted? If I'm put-ting up a fight. It's a
now he's down the crap-per While I'm work-ing in my prime. It's a

bus - 'ness. And I
bus - 'ness. And the

1.
want those pay-ing suck-ers out there Giv-ing me the bus - 'ness

ev - 'ry night! The

2.
shows I do do bus-'ness, 'Cause I real-ly know my bus-'ness, And I'm

giv - ing them the bus - 'ness, hon - ey All the time! To stage-hands, to the dres - sers to__ mu - si - cians in the pit,__ It's a bus - 'ness! The owner of these prem-is-es__ Cleans up if we're a hit,__ He's in bus-'ness!

Un-ion mem-bers Don't work for free__ Hey, Har-ry, on the spot-light, Blink twice if you a-

gree. See? I'm not devoid of culture But my feet are on the floor It's a bus-'ness! I'd do "The Kama Sutra" With a Richard Rodgers score. That's good

bus - 'ness! Yes, green's my fav-'rite col-or And I don't mean on the grass, It's a bus - 'ness! And the shows I do do bus-'ness Yes, I'm good at do-ing bus-'ness And if you don't like my bus-'ness, swee-tie, Blow it out your...

Bus - 'ness!

Bus - 'ness!

THINKING OF HIM
from *Curtains*

Music by JOHN KANDER
Lyrics by FRED EBB

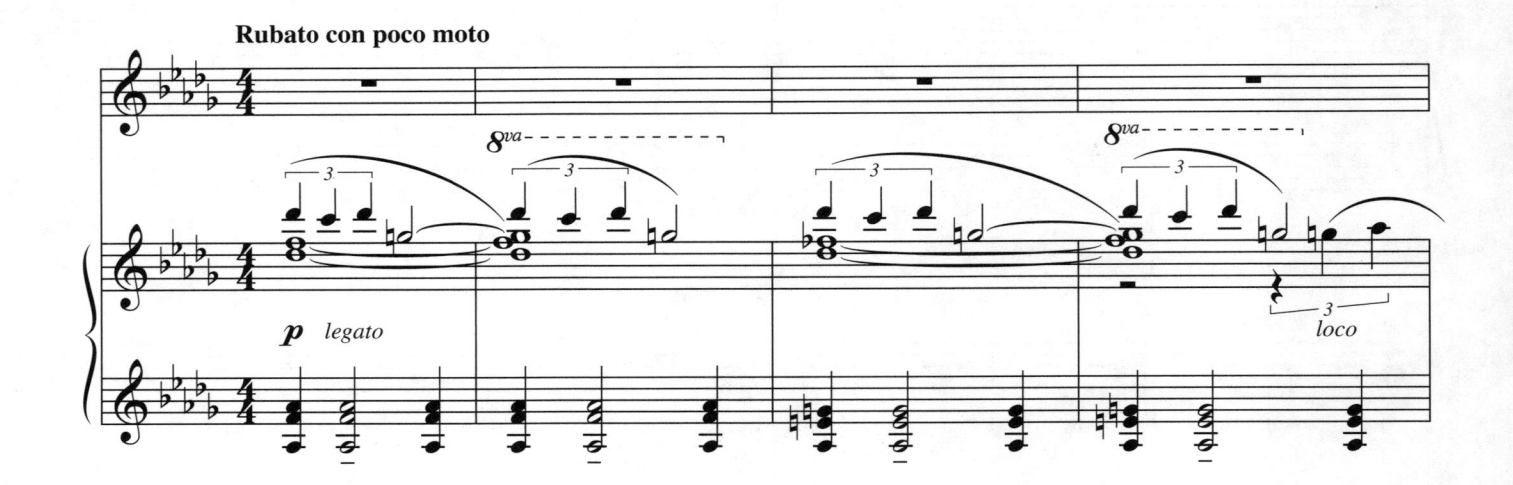

Rubato con poco moto

L'istesso tempo con poco moto

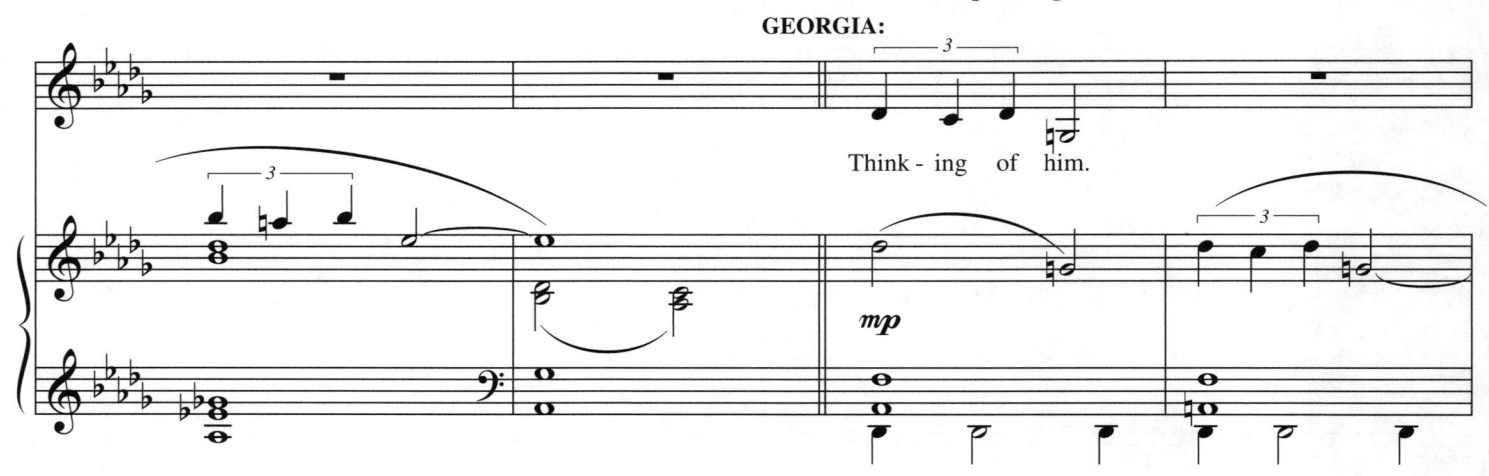

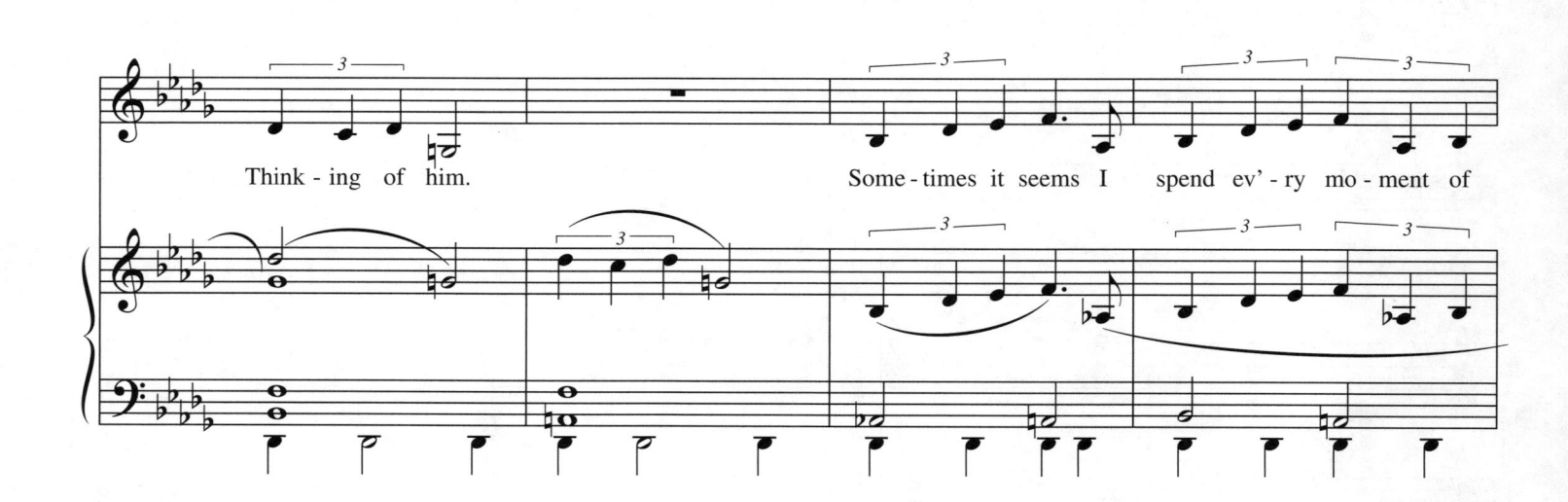

GEORGIA:
Think-ing of him. Think-ing of him. Some-times it seems I spend ev'-ry mo-ment of

Copyright © 1987, 2007 by Kander & Ebb, Inc.
All Rights Administered by Bro 'N Sis Music, Inc.
International Copyright Secured All Rights Reserved
Used by Permission

my wak-ing day. Think-ing of him. Mak-ing him laugh,

some-times. Mak-ing him strong, some-times. Mak-ing him feel some-

-place in the light is his. Tell-ing him just how spe-cial he is.

poco cresc. *poco rit.*

a tempo

Think-ing of him. Think-ing of him.

mf a tempo

Telling the truth when nobody's willing to tell him the truth. Fighting for him. Living for him, thinking it over, that's what I think I'll do. Well, isn't it time? Isn't it high time I was think - ing of me, _____ too? _____

May - be it's time. May - be it's high time _____

I was think - ing of _____ me, _____

too. _____

HERE I AM
from *Dirty Rotten Scoundrels*

Words and Music by
DAVID YAZBEK

Rubato

CHRISTINE: Would ya look at that coff-ered ceil-ing. Look at that chan-de-lier. Ex-cuse me, but how I'm feel-ing is a hun-dred proof. I could raise the roof I'm so hap-py to be here.

Copyright © 2004 David Yazbek
All Rights Reserved Used by Permission

Upbeat Latin (♩ = 103)

I've been kind of missing Mom and Daddy, sort of in a spin since Cincinnati. The morning flight, a major bore. But then they open the cabin door, and *zoot a-lors!* Here I am!

Lord knows I had the will and the resources. But Mom and Dad kept saying "hold your horses." I guess those ponies couldn't wait. Pardon me, folks, but they've left the gate. I may be late, but here I am!

Ah, the way to be, to me, is French. The way they *c'est la vie* is French. So here I am, Beaumont Sur Mer. A big two weeks on the Riviera. If I'm only dreaming, please don't wake me. Let the summer sun and breezes take

me.— Ex - cuse me if I seem *je - june,* I prom-ise I'll find my mar - bles soon. But, ev - 'ry-where I look, it's like a scene from a book. O - pen the book and here I am! I mean the air is French, that chair is French. This

nice sin-cere *Sancerre* is French, the skies are French, the pies are French, those guys are French, these fries are French. Pardon me if I fly off the handle, 'cause nowhere else on Earth can hold a candle. So *ve-ni vi-di vi-ci* folks Let's face it, *je suis ici* folks. *Excusez moi* if I spout, I'm letting my *je n' sais quoi* out. I'm sorry to shout, but here I am!

AND I AM TELLING YOU I'M NOT GOING
from *Dreamgirls*

Music by HENRY KRIEGER
Lyric by TOM EYEN

Moderately, in 2

EFFIE:
And I am tell-ing you I'm not go-ing. You're the best man I'll ev-er know. There's no way I can ev-er go, no, no, no, no way, no, no, no, no way I'm

livin' without you. I'm not livin' without you. I don't want to be free. I'm stayin', I'm stayin', and you, and you, you're gonna love me. Ooh, you're gonna love me. And I am tell-ing you I'm not go-ing, e-ven though the rough times are show-ing. There's just no way, there's no way. We're part of the same place.

G♭6
G♭maj7
G♭6
We're part of the same time. We
B♭(add2)
B♭6
B♭maj7
both share the same blood. We both have the same mind.
B♭6
Gm7
Gm7/F
And time and time we have so much to
f
B♭/C
C9
Cm7
share, no, no, no, no, no, no. I'm not wak - in' up to -
3
3
3
3

mor-row morn-in', and find-in' that there's no-bod-y there.

Dar-ling, there's no way, no, no, no, no way I'm liv-in' with-out you. I'm not liv-in' with-out you.

You see, there's just no way, there's no way.

Funky
E♭9
Gm7
Tear down the moun-tains, yell, scream and shout. You can say what you want, I'm not
E♭9
Cm7
3
walk-in' out. Stop all the riv-ers, push, strike, and kill. I'm
Freely
E♭/F
Cm/F
E♭maj7/F
E♭/F
F
not gon-na leave you, there's no way I will. And
rit.
Tempo I
E♭
F/E♭
I am tell - ing you I'm
rit.
mf

not go - ing. You're the best man I'll ev - er know. There's no way I can ev - er, ev - er go, no, no, no, no way, no, no, no, no way I'm liv - in' with - out you. Oh, I'm not liv - in' with - out you, I'm not liv - in' with - out you.

G♭ G♭6 B♭/C C9
I don't wan - na be free. I'm stay - in', I'm
B♭/C C9 E♭/F
stay - in', and you, and you, and you, you're gon - na love
B♭ B♭7/D♭ E♭ G♭6/A♭
me. Oh, hey, you're gon - na love
B♭ B♭7/D♭ E♭ G♭6/A♭
me. Yes, ah, ooh, ooh, love me,
3

B♭5
B♭7/D♭
B♭5
B♭7/D♭
ooh, ooh, ooh, love me,
love me,
love me,
p
f
p
f
B♭5
E♭sus2
B♭5
E♭m7
love me,
love ___ me.
mp
f
mf
f
Freely
N.C.
You're gon - na love
A♭6/9
C♭maj9
E♭/F
B♭
me.

I AM CHANGING
from *Dreamgirls*

Music by HENRY KRIEGER
Lyric by TOM EYEN

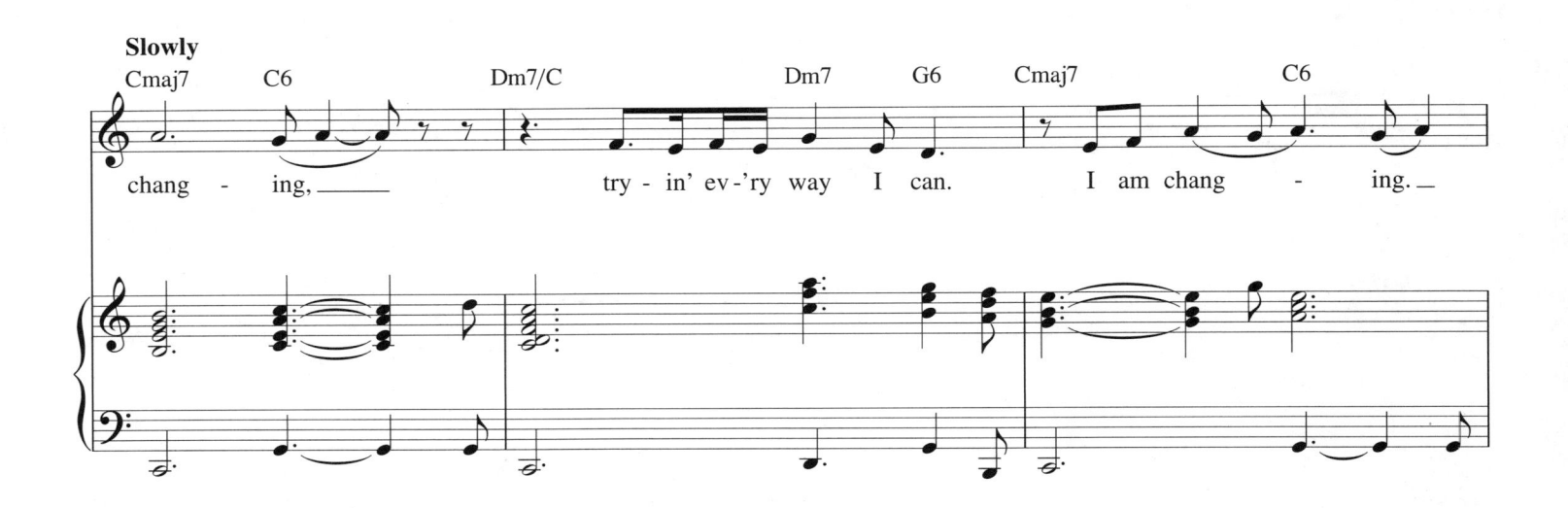

Freely

EFFIE: Look at me. Look at me. I am

Slowly

chang-ing, _____ try-in' ev-'ry way I can. I am chang-ing. _____

I'll ___ be bet-ter than I am. I'm try-ing

Copyright © 1981, 1982 UNIVERSAL - GEFFEN MUSIC, MIROKU MUSIC, UNIVERSAL - GEFFEN AGAIN MUSIC and AUGUST DREAM MUSIC LTD.
All Rights for MIROKU MUSIC Controlled and Administered by UNIVERSAL - GEFFEN MUSIC
All Rights for AUGUST DREAM MUSIC LTD. Controlled and Administered by UNIVERSAL - GEFFEN AGAIN MUSIC
All Rights Reserved   Used by Permission

Em7(add4) G/A A7(add13) Dm9 F
to find a way to un-der-stand. But I need you. I need you,
Dm7/G G7(add13) Cmaj7 C6
I need a hand. I am chang-ing,
Dm/C Dm7 G7(add13) Cmaj7 C6
see-in' ev-'ry-thing so clear. I am chang-ing.
Dm/C G6 Fmaj9
I'm gon-na start right now, right here. I'm hop-ing

Em7(add4) Em7 G/A A7
to work it out, and I know that I can. But I
Dm7 F Dm7/G G7(add13)
need you. I need a hand.
cresc.
A7sus D(add2)/A G6/A A7sus Adim A7(add13)
All of my life I've been a fool who said I could do it all a - lone.
f
G6/A A7sus D(add2)/A G6/A A7sus Adim
How man-y good friends have I al - read-y lost? How man-y dark nights have I known?

Walk-in' down that wrong road ____ there was noth-in' I could find.

All those years of dark-ness ____ could make a per-son bli-i-i-i-ind, but

now I can see I am chang-ing, ____ try-in' ev-'ry way I can.

I am chang-ing. ____ I'll ____ be bet-ter than I am. But I need ____ a friend ____

Em7 G/A F♯m/A A9 Dm7 Em7
to help me start all o - ver a - gain. Oh, that would be just fine.
gradual cresc.
Fmaj7 E7♯9(♭13) A7♯9(♭13) Dm7 Em7
I know it's gon-na work out this time, 'cause this time I am,
F F♯m7♭5 F6/G F/G N.C.
this time I am, I am
f
D♭maj7(add13) D♭6/A♭ E♭m/D♭ E♭m G♭/A♭
chang - ing. I'll get my life to-geth-er now. I

D♭maj7
D♭6/A♭
E♭m/D♭
E♭m
A♭
am chang - ing.
Yes, I know how.
I'm gon-na
G♭
Fm7
B♭13
B♭7♭9(♭13)
start a - gain.
I'm gon-na leave my past be - hind.
I'll
Slower
E♭m7
E♭m7♭5/A
G♭6/A♭
change my life.
I'll make a vow and noth - in's gon - na
G♭/A♭
G♭6/A♭
N.C.
D/D♭
D♭
stop me now!
molto rit.

SHOW OFF
from *The Drowsy Chaperone*

Words and Music by LISA LAMBERT
and GREG MORRISON

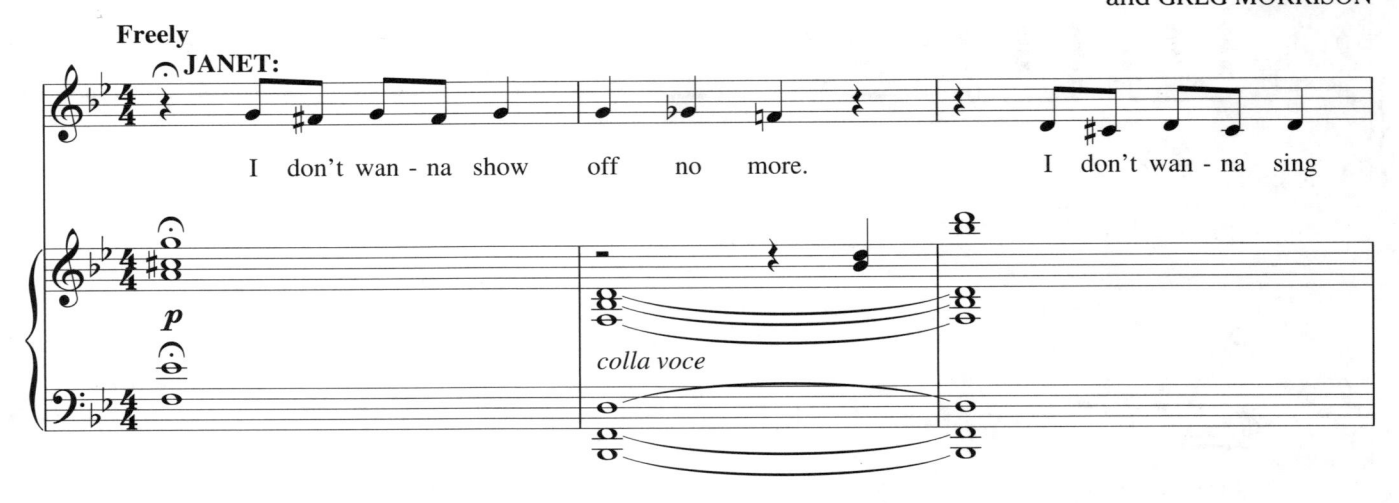

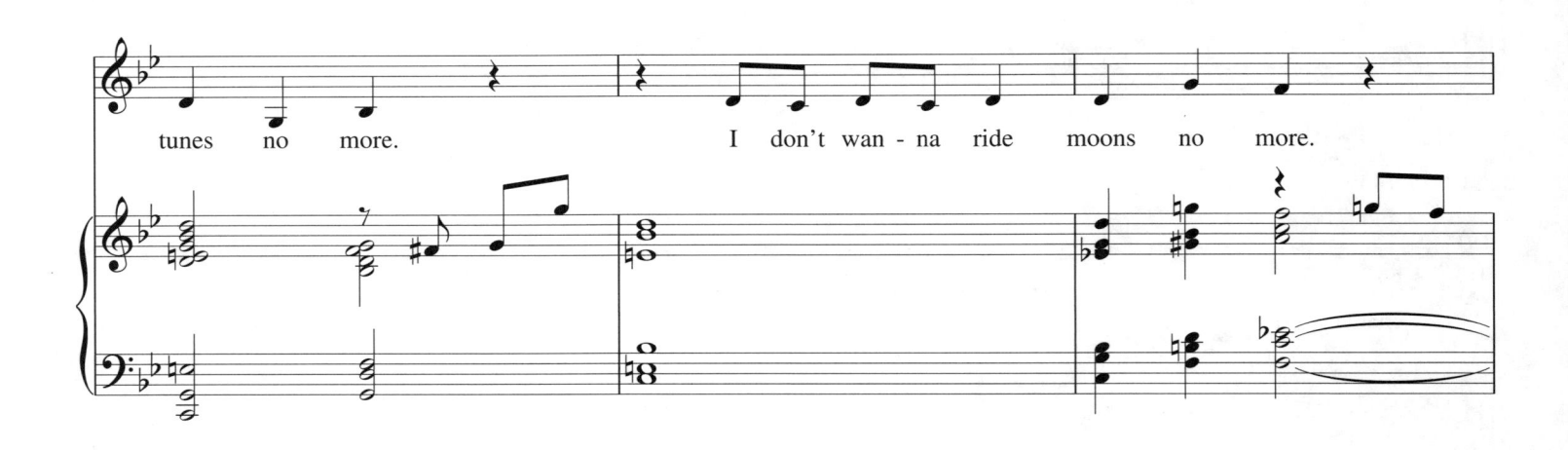

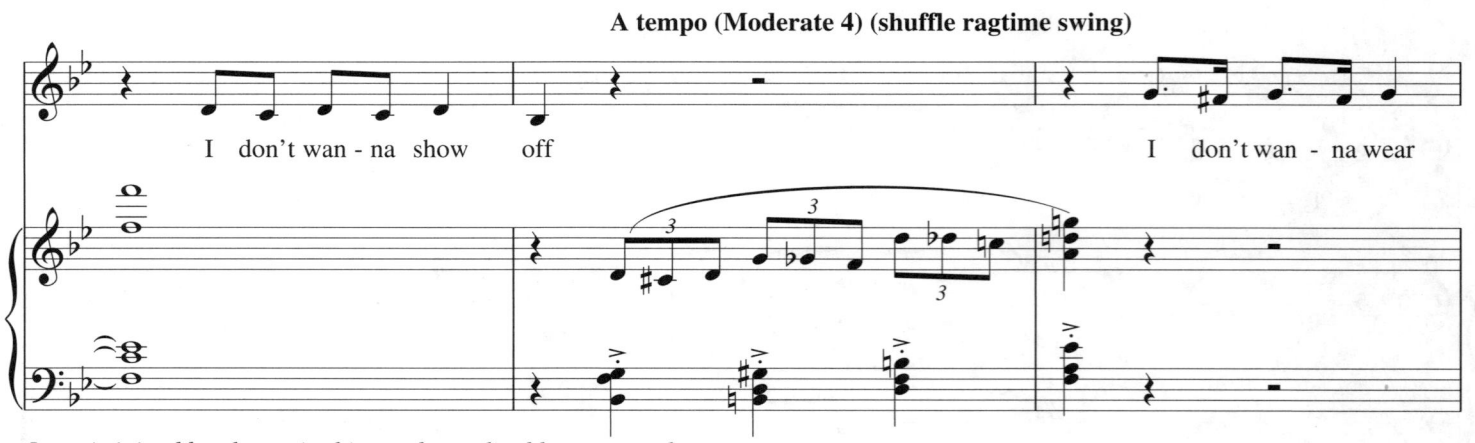

Freely

JANET: I don't wan-na show off no more. I don't wan-na sing tunes no more. I don't wan-na ride moons no more.

A tempo (Moderate 4) (shuffle ragtime swing)

I don't wan-na show off I don't wan-na wear

colla voce

Janet is joined by chorus in this number, edited here as a solo.

Copyright © 1999 Lisa Lambert and Gmorr Inc.
All Rights Reserved   Used by Permission

this no more___ play the sauc-y Swiss miss no more___ blow my sig-na-ture *(kiss)* no more. I don't wan-na show off. Don't try to con-trol me I've made up my mind And that's

it I quit I'm leaving it all behind

I don't wanna be cute no more Make the gentlemen hoot no more. I don't wanna wear fruit no more. I don't wanna show off. I don't wan - na show off no more __ Not me! read my name in the news no more, __ get the glow - ing re - views no more, Ah gee! I don't wan - na show off! I don't want to show off!

Wheee! Please no more at-ten-tion I've count-ed to ten and I'm thru. A-dieu You'll nev-er see this...

(she dances)

You'll

never see this...

(she dances again)

(teasing)

Never see this, never see that, never see these a-gain.

Pullback tempo

I don't wanna change keys no more, I don't wanna strip-tease no more. I don't wanna say cheese no more. I don't care if you scoff

I don't wan-na be cheered no more praised no more

grabbed no more touched no more loved no more I don't wan-na show

off I don't wan-na show off.

I don't wan - na show off.

I don't wan - na show

Faster

off!

no more!

FREDDY, MY LOVE
from *Grease*

Lyric and Music by WARREN CASEY
and JIM JACOBS

Moderately (♩. = 76)

MARTY:
Fred-dy, my love, I miss you more than words can say,

Fred-dy, my love, please keep in touch while you're a-way.

© 1971, 1972 WARREN CASEY and JIM JACOBS
© Renewed 1999, 2000 JIM JACOBS and THE ESTATE OF WARREN CASEY
All Rights Administered by EDWIN H. MORRIS & COMPANY, A Division of MPL Music Publishing, Inc.
All Rights Reserved

Hear-ing from you can make the day so much bet-ter, get-ting a sou-ve-nir or may-be a let-ter. I real-ly flipped o-ver the gray cash-mere sweat-er, Fred-dy, my love, Fred-dy, my love, Fred-dy, my love, Fred-dy, my lo-ove. Fred-dy, you know, your ab-sence makes me feel so

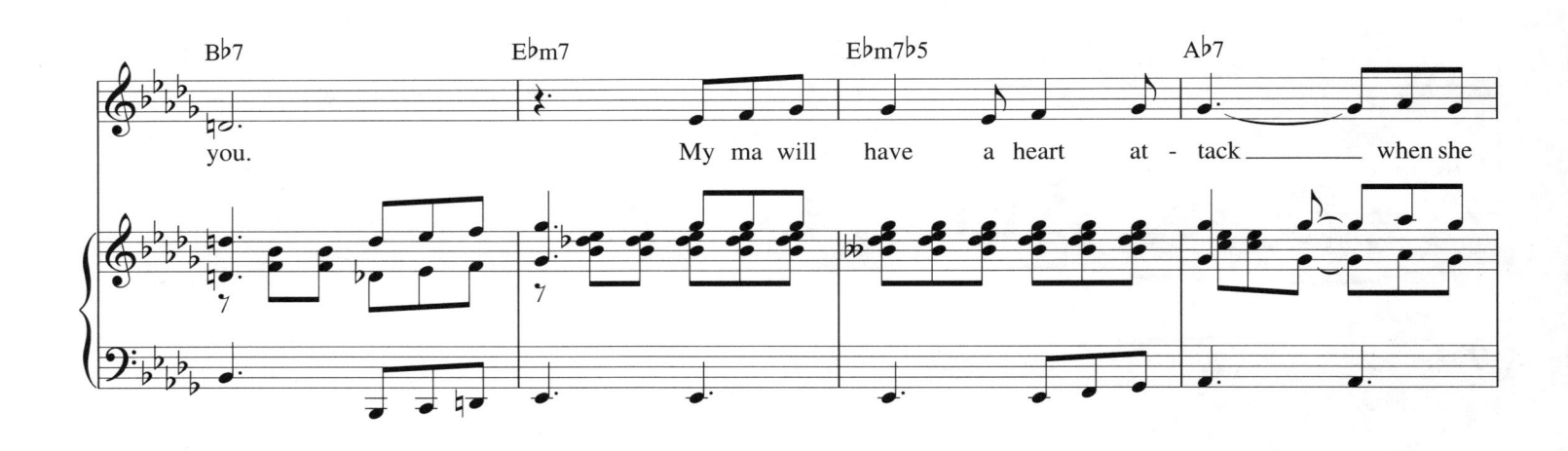

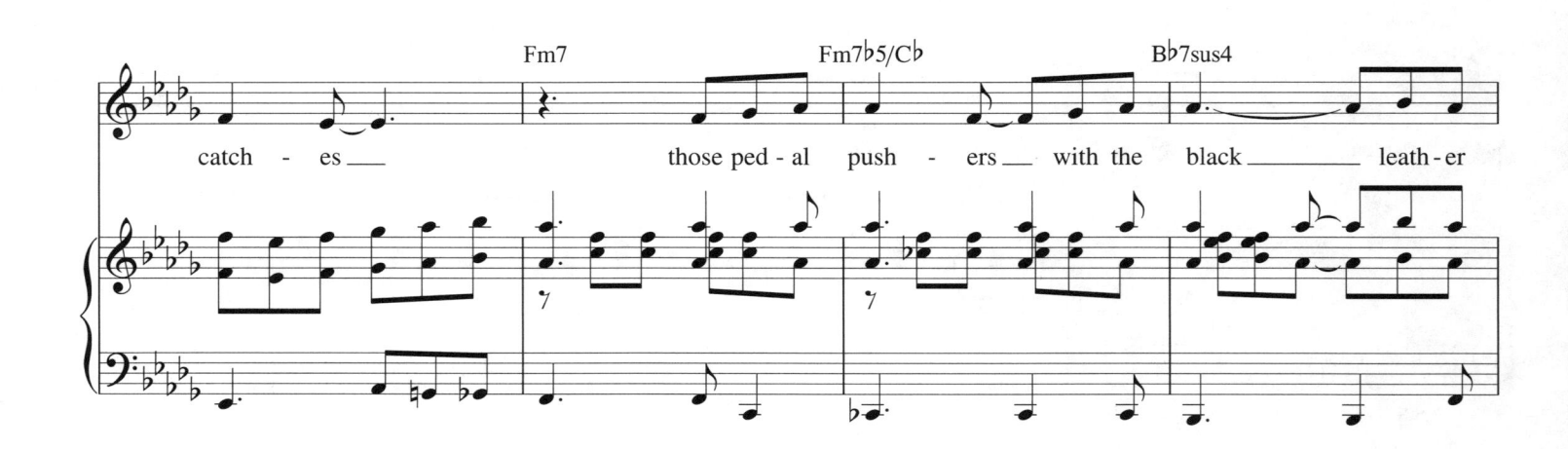

blue; that's o-kay, though, your pres-ents make me think of

you. My ma will have a heart at-tack when she

catch-es those ped-al push-ers with the black leath-er

patch - es.__ Oh, how I wish I had a jack - et that match - es, Fred-dy, my love, Fred-dy, my love, Fred-dy, my love, Fred-dy, my lo - ove.__ Don't keep your_ let-ters from me__ I thrill to__ ev-'ry line; your spell - ing's__ kind-a crum - my,__ but,

D♭m7 E♭m7♭5 A♭7
hon - ey, so is mine. I trea - sure ev - 'ry gift - ie, the
8vb
D♭m7 G♭7 C♭maj7
ring is real - ly nift - y, you say it cost you
B♭m7 E♭m7 A♭ E♭m7/A♭ D♭
fif - ty, so you're thrift - y, I don't mind, oohh, oh! Fred - dy, you'll
8vb
D♭maj7 D♭7 G♭ A♭7 D♭
see, you'll hold me in your arms some day; and I will

be wear-ing your lace-y___ loun-je-ray, think-ing a-bout it___ my heart's pound-ing al-read-y,___ know-ing when you come home, we're bound___ to go stead-y,___ and throw your ser-vice pay a-round___ like con-fet-ti, Fred-dy, my love, Fred-dy, my

D♭maj7 D♭7 G♭ A♭7 D♭ [start fade]
love, Fred - dy, my love, Fred - dy, my lo - ove. Fred - dy, my
D♭maj7 D♭7 G♭ A♭7
love, Fred - dy, my love, Fred - dy, my lo - ove.
D♭ D♭maj7 D♭7 G♭ A♭7
Fred - dy, my love, Fred - dy, my love, Fred - dy, my lo - ove.
rit.
D♭maj7
Fred - dy, my love.
f

THE CAKE I HAD
from *Grey Gardens*

Music by SCOTT FRANKEL
Lyrics by MICHAEL KORIE

Moderate Stride tempo

EDITH:

What good is cake you have but nev-er eat?

I nev-er could de-ny my-self a sweet, so I sliced my life and licked the knife, and ate the cake I had!

Copyright © 2006, 2007 by Staunch Music and Korie Music
Publishing and Allied Rights Administered by Williamson Music throughout the world
International Copyright Secured   All Rights Reserved

Two per-fect sons I thor-ough-ly en-joyed, an ab-sent spouse and cats to fill the void... and the tri-state's best ac-com-pan-ist, oh yes, I ate the cake I had! Moist! Light! Gai-ly dec-o-ra-ted! Ev-'ry tas-ty mor-sel, sa-vored, chewed and mas-ti-cat-ed!

Young! Bright! Rich and thin and clev-er! Like a sec-ond help-ing? sis-ter, would I ev-er!

The days are gone when mon-ey grew on trees. The Mon-ey Tree came down with Elm Dis-ease but at my age,_ ducks,_ for my two bucks,_ I'll eat the cake._ I have and like it. I'll eat the cake_ I have!

optional cut to **

continuing through the interlude

Gripe! Groan!_ Point_ the fa-mous fin-ger. Life_ is dis-sa-point-ing, put the par-ent through the wring-er. Sulk! Moan!_ Blame_ it on the moth-er. When_ I'm dead and bur-ied, you_ won't get an oth-er!

E-nough with all your cel-e-brat-ed loves. You had two hands. You could have mod-elled gloves. Is it my fault that your cake fell flat? That you're un-mar-ried, bald and fat? As the world waltzed by and

straight sixteenths

cresc. poco a poco

Ed - ie sat... I ate the cake I had and loved it! Oh, I ate the cake I had, no thanks to Dad - dy, I ate the cake I had!

GOOD MORNING BALTIMORE
from *Hairspray*

Music by MARC SHAIMAN
Lyrics by MARC SHAIMAN and SCOTT WITTMAN

1. Oh, oh, oh Woke up today feeling the way I always do.
2. Oh, oh, oh Look at my hair what "do" can compare with mine today?

Oh, oh, oh Hungry for something that I can't eat. Then I hear the beat, that rhythm of town starts
Oh, oh, oh I've got my hairspray and radio. I'm ready to go, the rats on the street all

Tracy is joined by the chorus in the original number, adapted here as a solo.

Copyright © 2000 by Winding Brook Way Music and Walli Woo Entertainment
All Rights Reserved   Used by Permission

calling me down. It's like a message from
dance 'round my feet. They seem to say Tracy, it's

high above. Oh, oh, oh Pulling me out to the
up to you. So, oh, oh Don't hold me back 'cause to-

smiles and the streets that I love! Good morning Baltimore!
day all my dreams will come true! Good morning Baltimore!

Ev-'ry day's like an o-pen door, Ev-'ry night is a
There's a flash-er who lives next door, There's a bum on his

Dsus D D/A Asus
fan - ta - sy, ev - 'ry sound's like a sym - pho - ny!
bar - room stool, they wish me luck on my way to school!
A D/A A7 Dsus(add2) D D/C
Good morn - ing Bal - ti - more And some day when I
G/B Gm/B♭ D/A
take to the floor the world's gon - na wake up and see
A D 1 A G D/A 2 D Dsus D D(add2) D
Bal - ti - more and me! I

know ev-'ry step, I know ev-'ry song. I know there's a place where
I be-long. I see all the par-ty lights shin-ing a-head, so
some-one in-vite me be-fore I ___ drop ___ dead! ___
So, oh, oh Give me a chance, 'cause when I start to dance, I'm a

Bm/A A G D D/F♯
mov - ie star! Oh, oh, oh Some-thing in - side of me
G♯m7♭5 E/G♯ F♯7♭9/A♯ Bm
makes me move, when I hear the groove, my moth - er says no but my
Gm/B♭ B♭7 D/A G♯m7♭5 E/G♯
feet tell me go! It's like a drum-mer in - side my heart!
D/A A D/A A D/A A D/A G D/G Em7/G Em7 B/G G
Oh, oh, oh Don't make me wait one more mo - ment for my life to

137

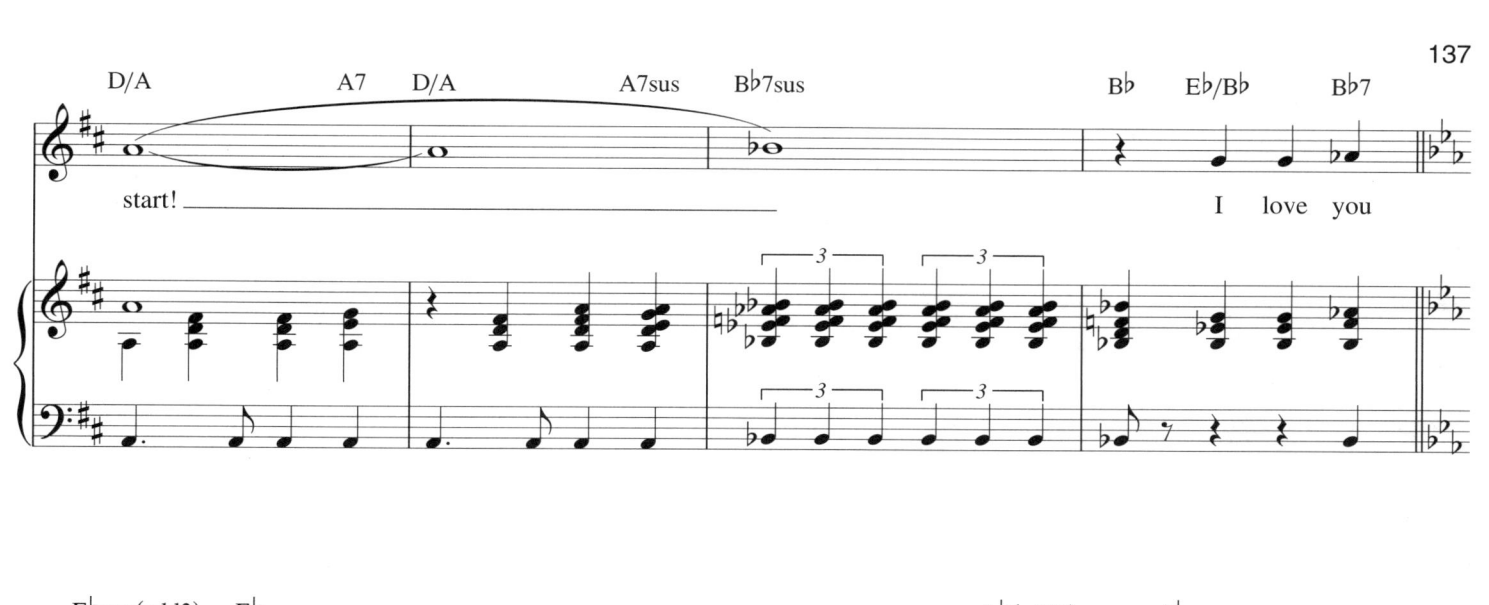

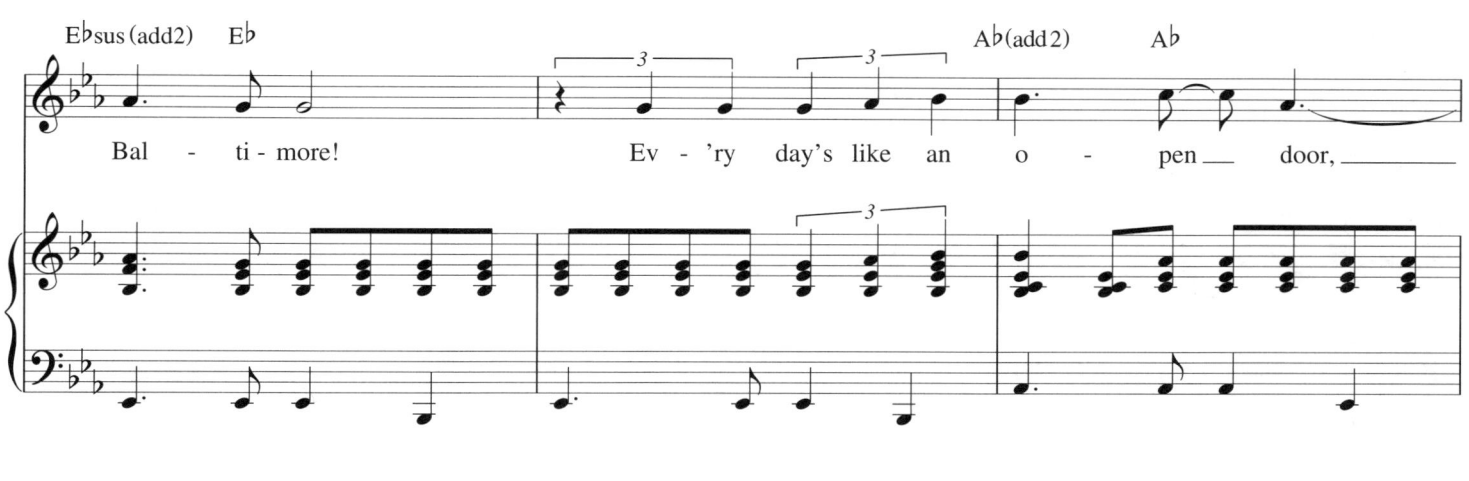

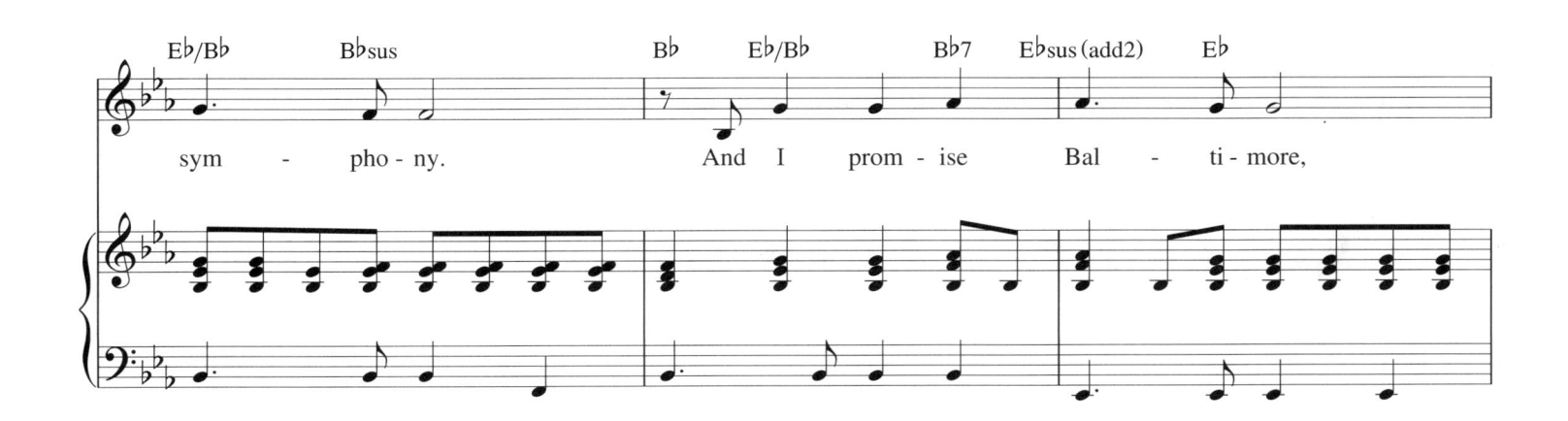

start! I love you Bal-ti-more! Ev-'ry day's like an o-pen door, ev-'ry night is a fan-ta-sy, ev-'ry sound's like a sym-pho-ny. And I prom-ise Bal-ti-more,

E♭/D♭
A♭/C
A♭m/C♭
that some - day when I take to the floor the world's gon - na wake up and
E♭/B♭
Am7♭5
A♭/B♭
B♭ A♭/B♭
see, gon - na wake up and see
B♭
E♭
E♭sus
E♭
E♭sus2
B♭
A♭/B♭ A♭ E♭/B♭
Bal - ti - more and me, Bal - ti - more and
E♭
E♭sus
E♭
E♭sus2
B♭
rit.
A♭/B♭ A♭ E♭/B♭
E♭
me, Bal - ti - more and me!
rit.

WHEN YOU COME HOME TO ME

from *The Last Five Years*

Music and Lyrics by
JASON ROBERT BROWN

Soon, a love will rise anew Even greater than the joy I've felt Just missing you, And once again, I'll be So proud to call you mine When fin-'lly you come home to *(Spoken:)* Thank you. Thank you so much."

I'm climbin' up hill, Daddy. Climbin' up hill. I'm up ev'ry morning at six And standing in line With two hundred girls Who are younger and thinner than me Who have

already been to the gym. I'm waiting five hours in line, And watching the girls Just coming and going In dresses that look just like this, 'Til my number is finally called. When I

walk in the room, There's a table of men Always men, usually gay — Who've been sitting, like I have, And list'ning all day To two hundred girls Belting as high as they can! I am a good per - son._____ I'm an at-trac-tive_ per - son!_____

I am_ a tal-ent-ed per - son!_____ Grant me

Grace!_____

Freely   **Moderately**
(conversationally - not strict)

When you come... home... I should have told them I was sick last week. They're gon-na think this is the way I sing. Why is the pi-an-ist play-ing so loud? Should I sing loud-er? I'll sing loud-er. May-be I should stop and start o-ver. I'm gon-na stop and start o-ver. Why is the dir-ec-tor star-ing at his crotch? Why is that man star-ing at my re-su-mé? Don't stare at my re-su-mé. I made up half of my re-su-mé. Look at me. Stop look-ing at that, look at me!

No, not at my shoes. Don't look at my shoes. I hate these fuck-ing shoes...

Why did I pick these shoes? Why did I pick this song? Why did I pick this ca-reer? Why

Molto rit.

A tempo

does this pi-an-ist hate me? If I don't get the

call-back, I can go to Crate and Bar-rel with Mom to buy a couch Not that I want to spend a day with Mom, but Jamie needs space to write, since I'm obviously such a horrible, annoying distraction to him. What's he gonna be like when we have kids? And once again... Why am I working so hard? These are the people who cast Linda Blair in a musical. Jesus Christ, I suck, I suck, I suck! When fin-'lly you come home To... *(Spoken:)* Okay, thank you.

Fast jig

I will not be the girl stuck at home in the 'burbs With the ba-by, the dog and a gar-den of herbs. I will not be the girl in the sen-si-ble shoes Push-ing bur-gers and beer nuts and miss-ing the clues. I will not be the girl who gets asked how it feels To be trot-ting a-long at the ge-nius-'s heels! I will not be the girl who re-quires a man to get by.

I CAN DO BETTER THAN THAT
from *The Last Five Years*

Music and Lyrics by
JASON ROBERT BROWN

Allegro

CATHERINE:
My best friend had a lit-tle sit-u-a-tion at the end of her sen-ior year,

And like a shot, she and Mitch-ell got mar-ried that sum-mer.

Copyright © 2002 by Jason Robert Brown
All Rights Controlled by Semolina Farfalle Music Co. Inc. (ASCAP)
International Copyright Secured   All Rights Reserved

Carol-ann gettin' bigger ev'ry minute, thinkin', "What am I doin' here?" While Mitchell's out ev'ry night bein' a heavy metal drummer. They got a little cute house on a little cute street With a crucifix on the door, Mitchell got a job at a record store in the mall. Just the typical facts of a typical life in a town on the Eastern shore. I thought about what I wanted, It wasn't like that at all... Made Carolann a cute baby sweater, thinkin' "I can do better than that."

In a year or so, I moved to the ci-ty, think-in', "What have I got to lose?"

Got a room, got a cat, and got twen-ty pounds thin-ner.

Met a guy in a class I was tak-ing who, you might say, looked like Tom Cruise.

He wouldn't leave me alone 'less I went with him to dinner. And I guess he was cute, and I guess he was sweet, and I guess he was good in bed: I gave up my life for the better part of a year. So I'm starting to think that this maybe might work, and the second it entered my head, He needed to take some time off, Focus on his "career." He blew me off with a heart-felt letter, I thought, "I can do better than that." You don't have to get a haircut, You don't have to change your shoes, You don't

have to like Du-ran Du-ran, just love me. You don't
have to put the seat down, You don't have to watch the news, You don't
have to learn to tan-go, You don't have to eat pro-sciut-to, You don't

crisper cresc. poco a poco

have to change a thing, Just stay with me!

B7sus B7 A/B D6/9
— I want you and you and noth-ing but you, Mi-
Bm11 G6/9 C7(♯11)
-les and pi-les of you Fi-nal-ly I'll have some-thing worth-while to think of each
8va loco
D2 G2
morn-ing: You and you and noth-ing but you! No
E7sus E9 G2 C7(♯11) C9
sub-sti-tu-tion will do, No-thing but fresh, un-di-lu-ted and pure, Top of the
mf

line, _____ And to-tal-ly _____ mine! _____

I don't need an-y life-time com-mit-ments, I don't need to get hitched to-night, _____

I don't want you to throw up all your walls _____ and _____ de-fens-es.

I don't mean to put on any pressure, but I know when a thing is right,
And I spend ev'ry day reconfiguring my senses. When we get to my house, take a look at that town, Take a look at how far I've gone. I will never go back, never look back anymore. And it feels

_ like my life led right_ to your side_ and will keep me there_from now_ on.

Think a-bout what you_ wan - ted, Think a-bout what could_ be,_____

Think a-bout how_ I____ love_ you_ and say__ you'll move in with_ me.

Think of what's great a-bout me and you,_ Think_ of the bull - shit we've both been through, Think_ of what's past, be-cause we can do Bet - ter!

We can do bet - ter!

We can do bet - ter than that!

We can do bet-ter than that!

MY BODY
from *The Life*

Music by CY COLEMAN
Lyrics by IRA GASMAN

Fast Funk ♩ = 152

I've had it up to here with all those "hol-i-er than thous" who want to save me from the dev-il's wick-ed den. When all they real-ly want is what those jok-ers al-ways want, and when they

This version has been adapted as a solo.

Copyright © 1996 Notable Music Company, Inc.
All Rights Administered by Chrysalis Music
All Rights Reserved   Used by Permission

get it, we don't see 'em 'til they want it a-gain. Don't quote me no com-mand-ments. Don't preach me no jive There's on-ly one com-mand-ment: Thou shalt sur-vive.

Maybe I'm a sinner, but who's gonna cast the first stone? It's my bod-y, and my bod-y's no-bod-y's bus-'ness but my own.

What if I'm a sinner? Hell, I ain't ex-act-ly a-lone. It's my bod-y and my bod-y's no-bod-y's bus-'ness but my own.

D♯7 C♯2/E♯ F♯m6 D♯7/G♮ D♯7 G♯m7
All those up - town la - dies look and dress so fine.
8vb
C♯7 D♯m♭5
They can sell it their
mf
Em6 C♯9/E♯ C♯m7/F♯ E/F♯
way, let me sell it mine.
B D♯7 G♯m7 F♯m7 B9
May - be you don't like it. May - be you don't like it, but

that don't mean noth-in', be - cause my bod - y is my bus - 'ness, my bus - 'ness, not yours.

I know what I'm do - ing. I know who I am.

C♯7 D♯m7 Em6 C♯9/E♯
If you got a prob - lem,
(8vb)
C♯m7/F♯ E/F♯
I don't give a damn.
B D♯7 G♯m7
Ain't no doubt a - bout it. Ain't
G9 F♯m7 B9 E F°7 F♯m7 B7
no doubt a - bout it,'cause ba - by it's writ - ten in stone. It's

my bod-y not your bod-y, and my bod-y is my bus-'ness. My bus-'ness is my bus-'ness, no-bod-y's bus-'ness, no-bod-y's bus-'ness, bus-'ness, but my own!

LIVE OUT LOUD
from *A Little Princess*

Music by ANDREW LIPPA
Lyrics by BRIAN CRAWLEY

Gentle, but with a strong sense of time

(slightly ad lib. at first)

I don't want to go a - long with the crowd. Don't want to live life un - der a cloud. Give me some air and space and the

articulation simile

a tempo (♩= 112)

sun on my face. I want to live out loud. Don't want to be

a tempo

Copyright © 2004 LippaSongs and crawleymuse(sic)
All Rights Reserved Used by Permission

a - lone in the crowd. Don't want to seem pe - cu - liar and proud.

I need to be as free as I know how to be.

Playful

I want to live out loud.

Ev - 'ry day. Sleep - walk, lock - step, no one dares to stray.

simile

Though they may, straight-laced, shame-faced, long to break away. They're as lonely as can be. Is that what they want from me? I don't want to go along with the crowd. Don't want to live life un-der a cloud. Give me some air and space and the sun on my face. I want to live out loud. Don't want to be a-lone in the crowd. Don't want to seem pe-cu-liar and proud. No-bod-y wants me here, but I won't dis-ap-pear.

Quasi African Drums

I want to live out loud.

I want to run down an o-pen shore-line. I want to join in a moon-lit dance.

I want to swing in the branch-es of a tree.

I want to bathe in a hid-den in-let and let the breeze come and dry my hair.

I want the life they took a-way from me! If that makes me head-strong, fine. That's a fault I'm glad is mine. I don't want to go a-long with the crowd. Don't want my spir-it bro-ken and bowed. Why do I have to hide____ what I'm feel-ing in - side?___ I want to live___ out loud.___

Don't want to be___ a - lone___ in the crowd.___ I on-ly want___

___ what I'm___ not al - lowed.___ Give me the wings___ of a bird,___ I'll be seen and be heard. I want to sing when my heart is full. I want to sing and I want to fly.

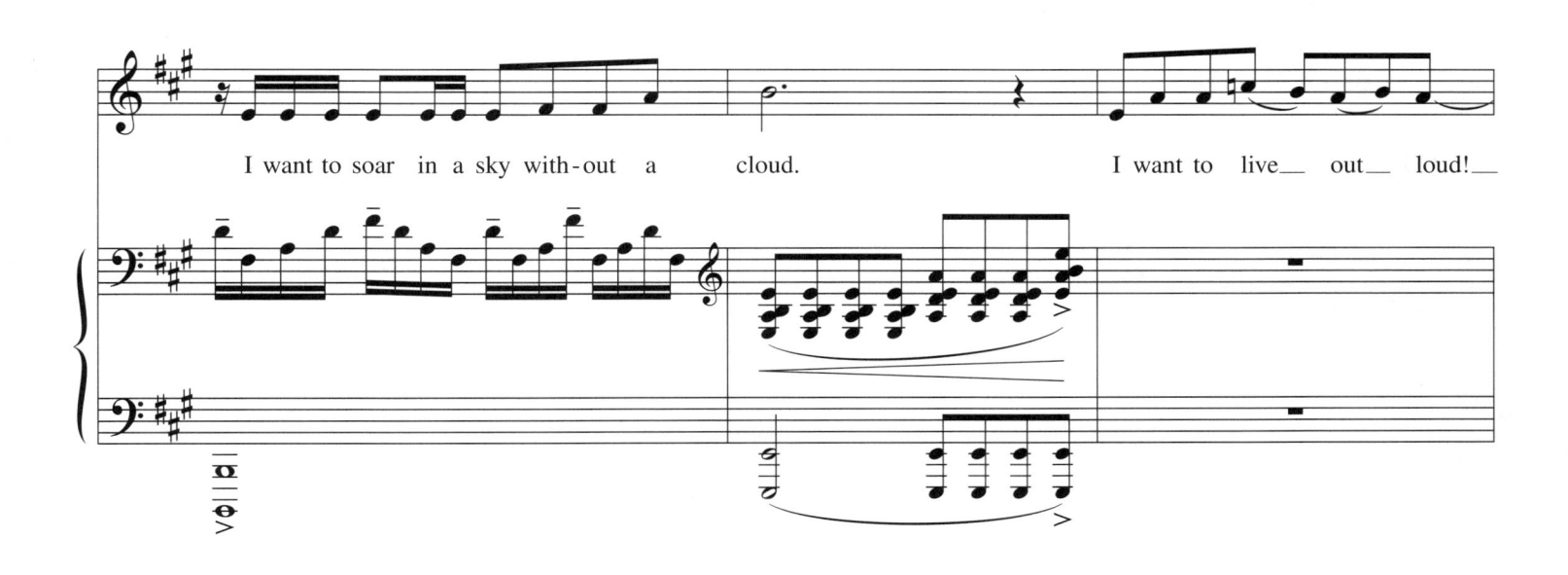

same as before

I want to soar in a sky without a cloud. I want to live out loud!

ff

THE WINNER TAKES IT ALL
from *Mamma Mia!*

Words and Music by BENNY ANDERSSON and BJÖRN ULVAEUS

Moderato (♩ = 124)

I don't wan-na talk a-bout things we've gone through. Though it's hurt-ing me, now it's his-to-ry. I've played all my cards. And that's what you've done, too.

Copyright © 1980 UNION SONGS MUSIKFORLAG AB
All Rights in the United States and Canada Controlled and Administered by UNIVERAL - SONGS OF POLYGRAM INTERNATIONAL, INC.
and EMI WATERFORD MUSIC, INC.
All Rights Reserved   Used by Permission

nothing more to say, no more ace to play. The winner takes it all. The loser standing small beside the victo- ry— that's her destiny.

I was in your arms, thinking I belonged there. I figured it made sense, building me a fence, building me a home. Thinking I'd be strong there.

*Because the song is rather long as a solo, a possible cut could be taken to **.

But I was a fool, playing by the rules. The Gods may throw a dice, their minds as cold as ice, and someone way down here loses someone dear.

The winner takes it all, the loser has to fall. It's simple and it's plain— why should I complain? But tell me: Does she kiss like I used to kiss you? Does it feel the

same when she calls your name? Somewhere deep inside you must know I miss you. But what can I say? Rules must be obeyed. The judges will decide, the likes of me abide. Spec-ta-tors of the show al-ways stay-ing low. The game is on a-gain, a lov-er or a friend, a big thing or a small, the win-ner takes it

all. _____ I don't wan-na talk 'cause it makes me feel sad. ___ And I un-der-stand you've come to shake my hand. I ___ a-pol-o-gize if it makes you

mp simply

with growing intensity

C♯/E♯
G♯m/D♯
feel bad seeing me so tense,
C♯
no self-confidence. But you see, the winner takes it
F♯
B♭7/D
D♯m
all,
E♭7/G
G♯m
the winner takes it all.

The game is on a-gain, a lov-er or a friend, a big thing or a small, the win-ner takes it all, the win-ner takes it all.

HURRY! IT'S LOVELY UP HERE

from *On a Clear Day You Can See Forever*

Words by ALAN JAY LERNER
Music by BURTON LANE

Slowly

Moderately - in an easy 4

DAISY:
Hey, buds be-low, Up is where to grow, Up, with which be-low can't com-pare with. Hur-ry, it's love-ly up here.

Copyright © 1965 by Chappell & Co. and WB Music Corp. in the United States
Copyright Renewed
Chappell & Co. owner of publication and allied rights for the rest of the world
International Copyright Secured   All Rights Reserved

Life down a hole Takes an aw-ful toll, What with not a soul there to share with. Hur-ry, it's love-ly up here.

Wake up! Be-stir your-self. It's time that you dis-in-ter your-self. You've got a spot to fill; A pot to fill.

And what a gift package of show-er, sun and love You'll be met a-bove ev-'ry-where with. Fon-dled and sniffed by mill-ions who drift by. Life here is ro-sy If you're a po-sy. Hur-ry! It's

rall.

love-ly here.

Hey, rho-do-dend! Cour-age, lit-tle friend. Ev-ry-thing 'll end rho-do-dan-dy. Hur-ry! It's love-ly up here. Climb up, ge-

ra-ni-um, It can't be fun sub-ter-ra-ne-um. On the ex-ter-i-or, It's cheer-i-er. R. S. V. P., pe-on-ies, Pol-in-ate the breeze. Make the queen of bees hot as bran-dy. Come give at least a Pre - view of East - a

Come up and see the hoot we're giv-ing. Come up and see the grounds for liv-ing. Come poke your head out. O-pen up and spread out. Hur-ry, it's love-ly here.

WOMAN
from *The Pirate Queen*

Music by CLAUDE-MICHEL SCHÖNBERG
Lyrics by ALAIN BOUBLIL, RICHARD MALTBY, JR.
and JOHN DEMPSEY

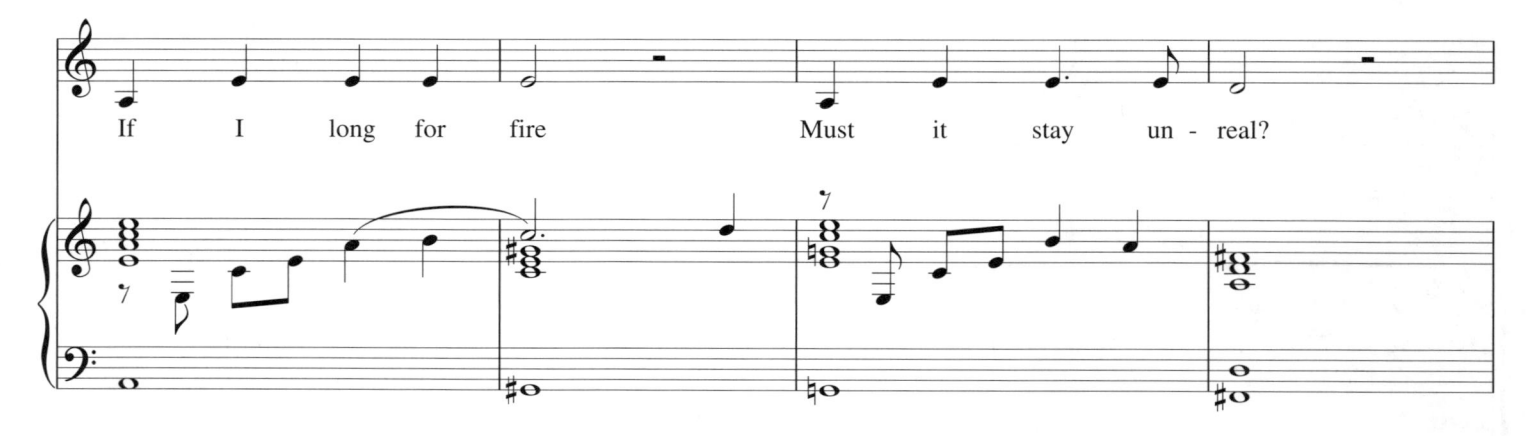

Moderately slow

mf

GRANIA:
Wom-an I am born What does "wom-an" mean?
Must my dreams face scorn? Held back and un-seen.
If I long for fire Must it stay un-real?

Copyright © 2005, 2006, 2007 by Bouberg Music Ltd.
Mechanical and Publication Rights for the U.S.A. Administered by Alain Boublil Music Ltd. (ASCAP) c/o Joel Faden & Company, Inc.,
1775 Broadway, Suite 708, New York, NY 10019, Tel. (212) 246-7203, Fax (212) 246-7217, E-mail mwlock@joelfaden.com
International Copyright Secured. All Rights Reserved. This music is copyright. Photocopying is illegal.
All Performance Rights Restricted.

Can I not de-sire? Am I not to feel?

If I ache to taste Am I not to try?

If my heart says sail Why should I de-ny?

I have my dreams, I have made plans I see hori - zons wide as a man's. Must I be noth - ing 'til I'm some man's wife? Look at this face, Does it de - ceive? Do I look made to milk and to weave? I will be damned to hell if that is my life.

I'm al - most your age, I'm your match in size.

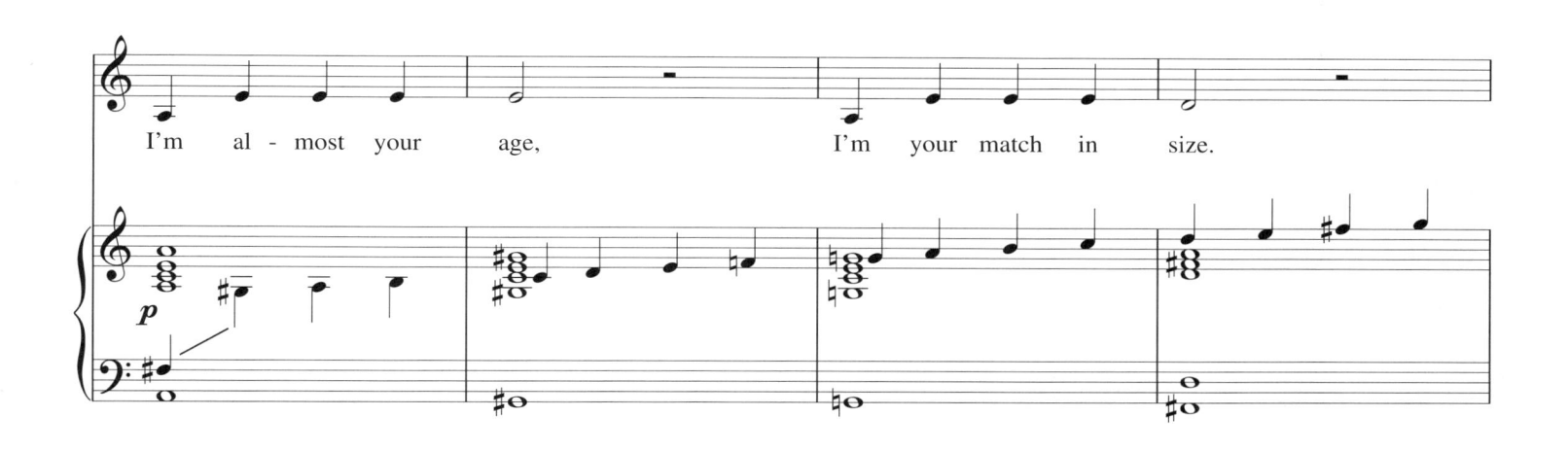

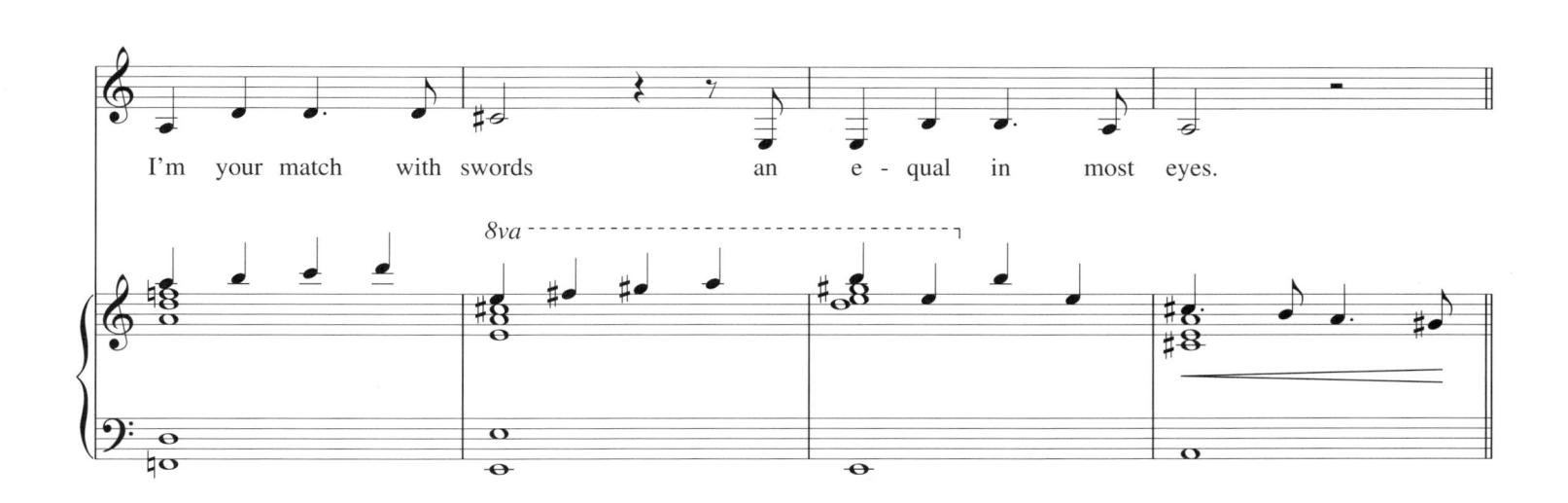

I'm your match with swords an e - qual in most eyes.

But when you have a dream And you're caught in its grip You can climb a-board a ship, You can, You can for you're a man. You can reach toward that place Where the earth meets the sky.

Fight a bat-tle, be brave, be true, If you can do it, Why not I? _____ I'm meant to fly Sail un-re-strained Why is man free and wom-an chained? Is that my ep-i-taph be-fore I die? I should be free, Free to be

Grace, I want to feel the wind on my face! And when life beck-ons, I should go, Face out the storm, Not stay be-low, Am I to be just wom-an? No, Not I.

TAKE THAT LOOK OFF YOUR FACE
from *Song and Dance*

Music by ANDREW LLOYD WEBBER
Lyrics by DON BLACK

Moderately ♩ = 104

I can't quite be-lieve it, I'm
all, so a-maz-ing, the

ac-tual-ly here, the one place on earth I want to be.
size and the noise. Why, it's still a-live at five a.m.

New York is just short of per-
And that drive in the eyes of

© Copyright 1980 Andrew Lloyd Webber licensed to The Really Useful Group Ltd. and Universal/Dick James Music Ltd.
All Rights for Universal/Dick James Music Ltd. in the U.S. and Canada Controlled and Administered by Universal - PolyGram International Publishing, Inc.
International Copyright Secured   All Rights Reserved

fec-tion they say. The one thing it lacks is me. It's
New York girls, oo, I'd like to be one of them.

Take that look off your face. What's the
joke, if you please? Oh, I knew what you'd say, Eng-lish
girls come by plane loads each day and you fear that I'll

lose my-self like so man-y do. Well, I've got news for you:

I'm fright-ened too. I'm glad to have you, Viv, a friend o-ver here who's had a whole year to learn the ropes. This guy that I'm with, this drum-mer from Queens, he's cra-zy, but I have hopes. Take that look off your face. Oh, I knew how you'd be. You think I'm the same girl who lets men take ad-vantage of me, here's one more. And he's pos-si-bly us-ing me, it's

true. Still, I'm here in New York; Who's us-ing who?! Take that look off your face. Don't go off in a tizz. I am here to have fun finding out what A-mer-i-ca is. Can't you

see I'm no long-er the mess I used to be. You're my best friend and yet, you don't know me. So get used to me here. I am gon-na work hard, get my card, have a bril - liant ca - reer, ___ stay in love, and out-

shine an - y New York girl you'd see. If you think that I won't,

you don't know me! ___

WITHOUT YOU
from *Rent*

Words and Music by
JONATHAN LARSON

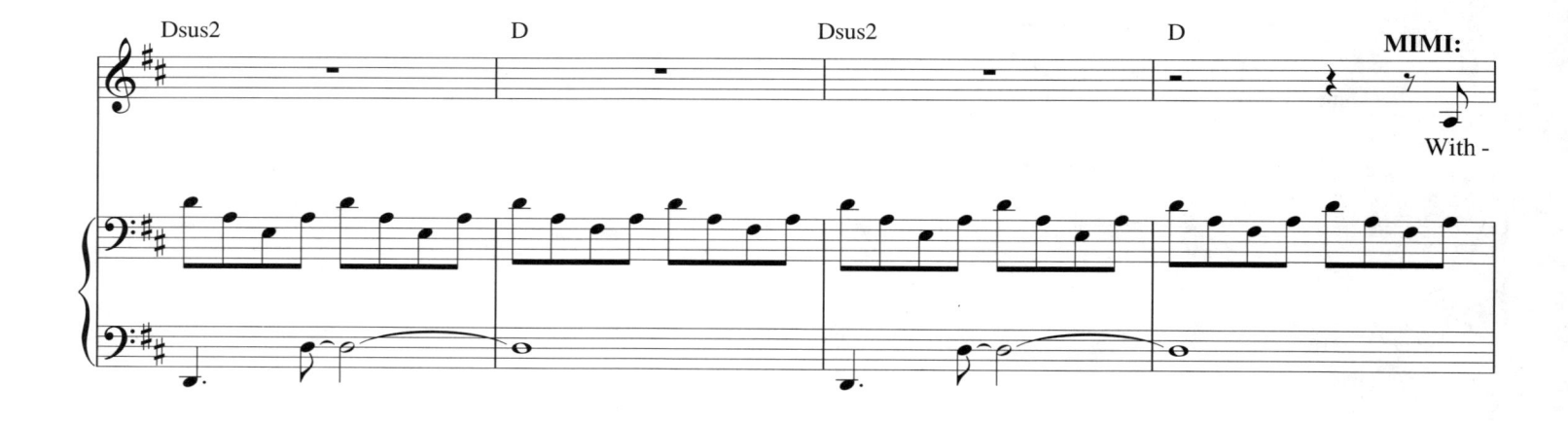

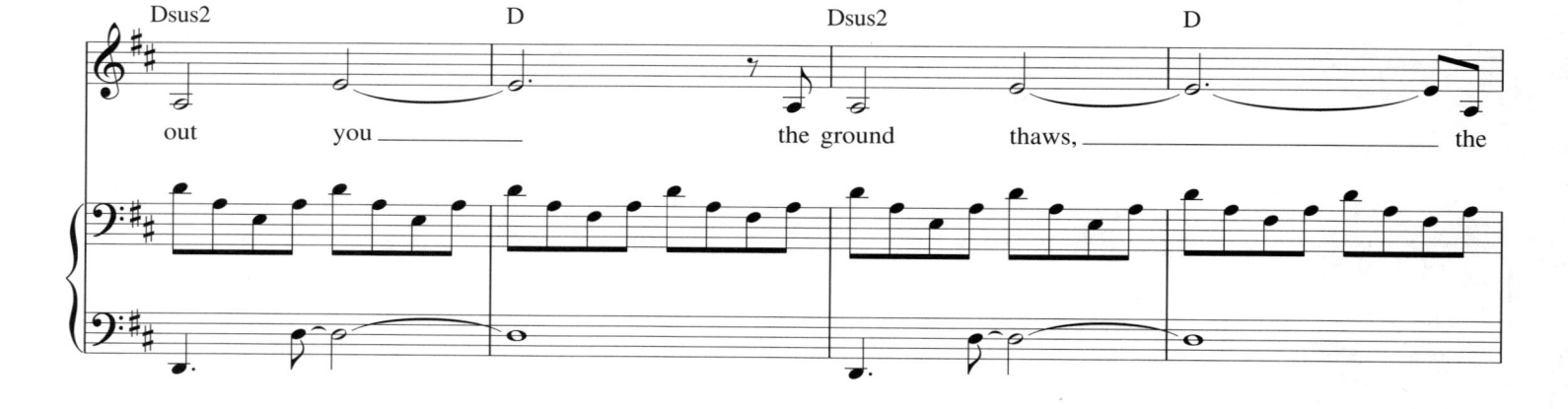

Moderate Rock Ballad ♩ = c. 66

MIMI: With- out you ___ the ground thaws, ___ the rain falls, ___ the grass grows. ___ With-

This song for Mimi and Roger has been adapted as a solo for this edition.

Copyright © 1996 FINSTER & LUCY MUSIC LTD. CO.
All Rights Controlled and Administered by UNIVERSAL MUSIC CORP.
All Rights Reserved   Used by Permission

out you_____ the seeds root,_____ the flow-ers bloom,_____ the chil-dren play,_____ the stars gleam,_____ the po-ets dream,_____ the ea - gles fly. With - out you the earth turns, the sun burns, but I die with - out you.

211

tides change, the boys run, the o-ceans crash, the crowds roar, the days soar, the ba-bies cry. With-

Dsus2 D Dsus2 D Bm7sus Bm7
out you the moon glows,
Gsus2 Bm7sus Bm7 Gsus2
the riv - er flows, but
F♯m Gsus2 Dsus2
I die with - out you.
D Dm7 Dsus2
mf
The world re - vives,

Dm7
Dsus2
Dm7
col - ors re - new
but I know
A/C♯
Am/C
G/B
blue,
on - ly
blue,
Gm/B♭
D/A
lone - ly
blue,
with - in me
A
rit.
Dsus2
a tempo
D
blue
with - out
you.
rit.
p
a tempo

With-out you the hand gropes, the ear hears, the pulse beats. With-out you the

Dsus2
D
Dsus2
eyes gaze, the legs walk,
D
Dsus2
D
the wings breathe, the
Bm7sus
D/G
Bm7sus
mind churns, the mind churns, the heart yearns, the heart
mf
D/G
F♯m
Gsus2
yearns, the tears dry with-
(over R.H.)

out you. Life goes on, but I'm gone, 'cause I die with-out you, with-out you, with-out you.

HIT ME WITH A HOT NOTE
from *Sophisticated Ladies*

Words and Music by DUKE ELLINGTON
and DON GEORGE

Medium Swing

[walking bass, detached]

(soprano head voice)

Hit me with a hot note and watch me bounce.

opt.

Hit me, hit me with a hot note and watch me bounce.

(belt voice)

Hit me with a hot note and watch me bounce. Hit

This standard can be done various ways. This arrangement is based on the version performed in Sophisticated Ladies.

Copyright © 1945 (Renewed 1973) by Famous Music LLC and Ricki Music Company in the U.S.A.
Rights for the world outside the U.S.A. Controlled by EMI Robbins Catalog Inc. and Alfred Publishing Co., Inc.
International Copyright Secured   All Rights Reserved

C6 Am7 F6 G13 C6 C6/E
me with a hot note and watch me bounce. When trum-pets heat up,
F6 F♯dim7 C6/9/G G13 C6
Gim-me a rug to beat up. Hit me with a hot note and watch me bounce. Hit
Am7 F6 G13 C6 Am7
me with a hot note and watch me burn, Slap me down the rhy-thm from stem
F6 G13 C6 C6/E F6 F♯dim7
to stern. When sax-es flare up How can I keep my hair up?

Hit me with a hot note and watch me bounce. Start that trombone slid-in'
While I gather steam. Keep that tempo rid-in' And I'll
come in right on the beam. Hit me with a hot note and watch
me bounce; Knock me out with music in great a-mounts. Oh,

C6/9
F7
F♯dim7
C6/9/G
let that beat _ wave, We're gon-na have a heat wave. Hit me with a hot note and watch _
G9
C6
Gm7
C9
Fmaj9
_ me bounce. _ Start that trom - bone slid - in' While I gath - er steam. _
D7♭9
D13
G9
cresc.
_ Keep that tem - po rid - in', rid - in',
cresc.
A♭9
_ keep it rid - opt. in'. Hit _

Db6/9 Db6/9/F Gb9 Ab13 Db6/9 Db6/9/F
f
me with a hot note and watch me bounce, Knock me out with mu-sic in great
8vb
Gb9 Ab9 Db6/9 Db6/9/F Gb6 Eb7/G
a - mounts. Oh, let that beat wave, We're gon-na have a heat wave.
(8vb)
Db6/9/Ab
mp
(Bb9)
Hit me, ooh, yeah, hit me with a hot note. Hit
(8vb)
[walking bass, detached]
(Eb7) (Ab7) (Ebm7) (Eb7) (Db)
me with a hot note and watch me bounce.

FIND YOUR GRAIL
from *Monty Python's Spamalot*

Lyrics by ERIC IDLE
Music by JOHN DU PREZ and ERIC IDLE

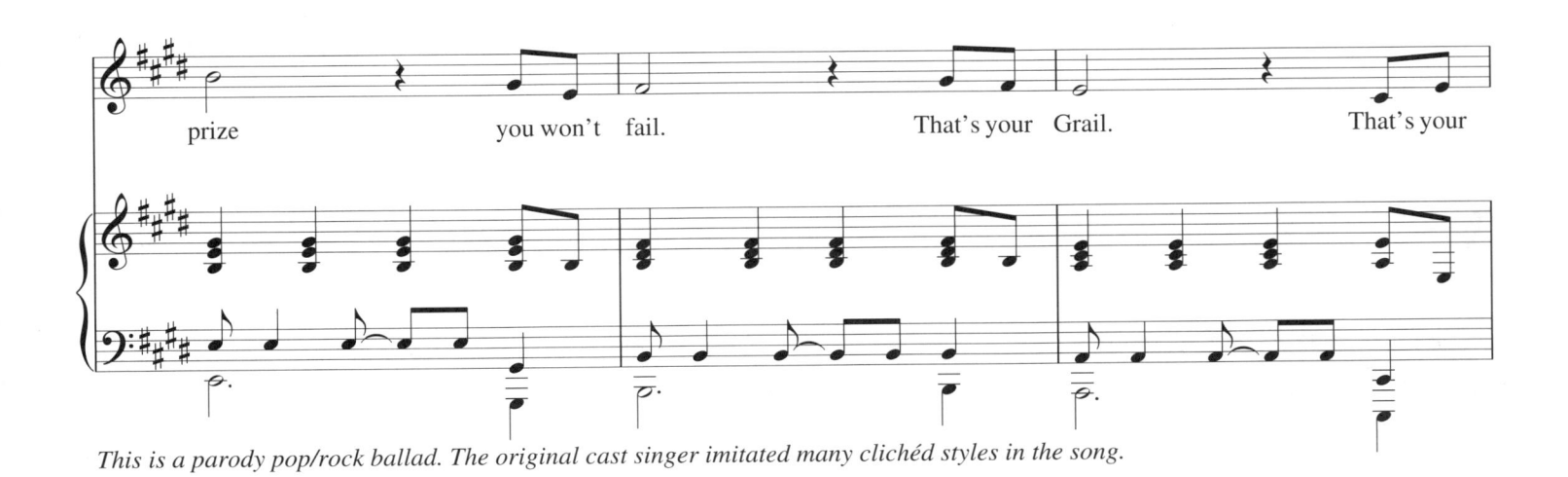

Pop Ballad, in 4

LADY OF THE LAKE: If you trust in your soul, keep your eyes on the goal. Then the prize you won't fail. That's your Grail. That's your

This is a parody pop/rock ballad. The original cast singer imitated many clichéd styles in the song.

Copyright © 2005 Rutsongs Music and Ocean Music LA Inc.
All Rights Reserved   Used by Permission

Grail So be strong. Keep right on to the end of your song Do not fail Find your Grail Find your Grail. Find your Grail. Life is real-ly up to you. You must choose what to pur-sue.

Set your mind on what to find, and there's nothing you can't do. So keep right to the end. You'll find your goal, my friend. You won't

fail. Find your Grail. Find your Grail. Find your Grail. Life is really up to you. You must choose what to pursue. Set your mind on what to find, And there's nothing you can't do, you can't

from here to the end Lady of the Lake improvises as an over-the-top pop diva.

do... So keep right to the end. You'll find your goal, my friend. You won't fail. Find your Grail. Find your Grail. Find your Grail.

ff *a tempo*
poco rall.
rall.

THE DARK I KNOW WELL

from *Spring Awakening*

Music by DUNCAN SHEIK
Lyrics by STEVEN SATER

Moderately fast, with intensity

MARTHA: There is a part I can't tell 'bout the dark I know well.

You say, "Time for bed now, child."

Sung by various characters (as indicated), the song can be sung as a solo.

Copyright © 2006 by Universal Music - Careers, Duncan Sheik Songs, Happ Dog Music and Kukuzo Productions, Inc.
All Rights for Duncan Sheik Songs and Happ Dog Music Administered by Universal Music - Careers
International Copyright Secured   All Rights Reserved

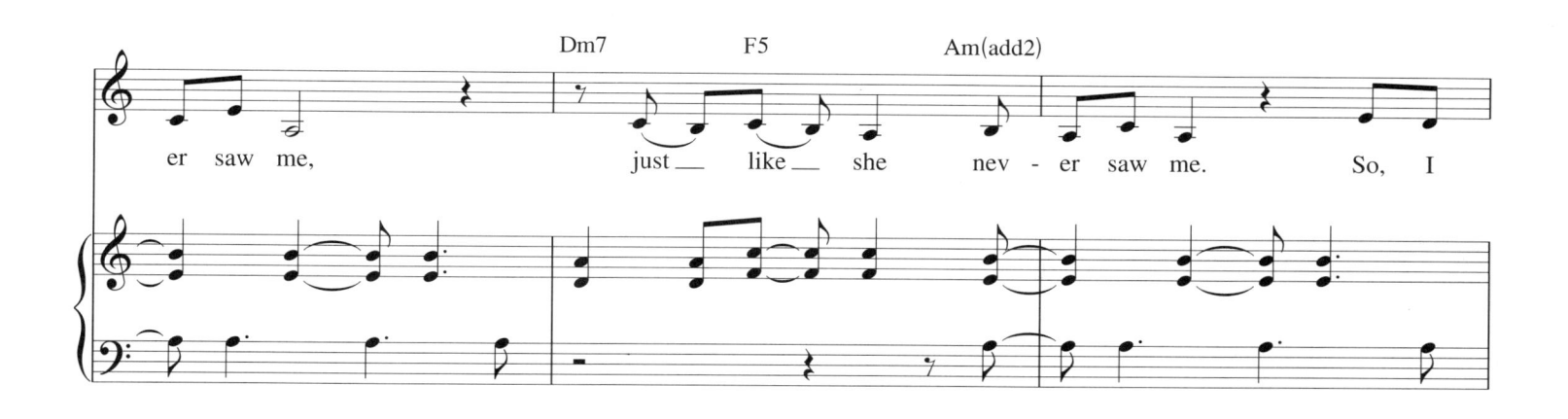

Mom just smiles that smile, just like she never saw me, just like she never saw me. So, I leave, wantin' just to hide, knowin' deep inside you are comin' to me,

230

you are _ com-in' to _ me... You say all _ you want is just a kiss _

MORITZ, OTTO, GEORG, MALE ENSEMBLE:
(2nd time only) Ah _

_ good-night, _ then you hold _ me and you whis-per, "Child, the Lord won't _ mind. It's just you _
ah _

_ and me. Child, _ you're a beau-ty. _
Child, _ you're a beau-ty. _

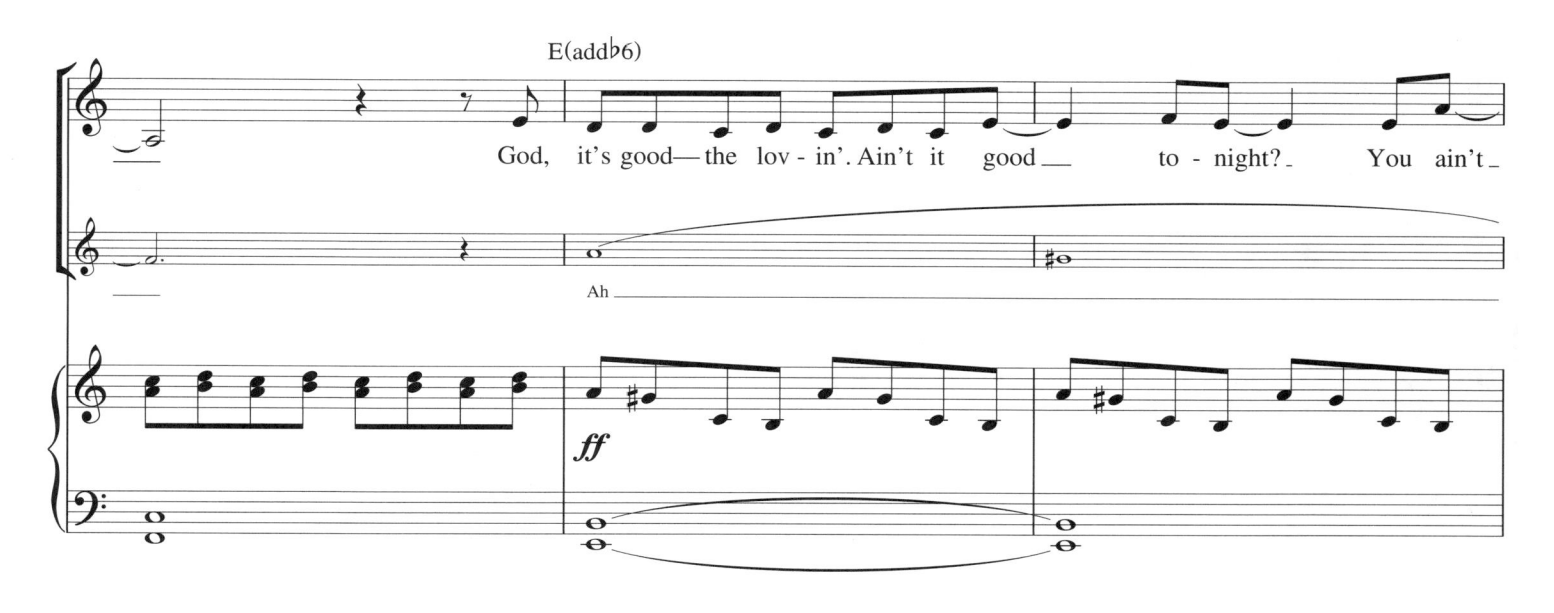

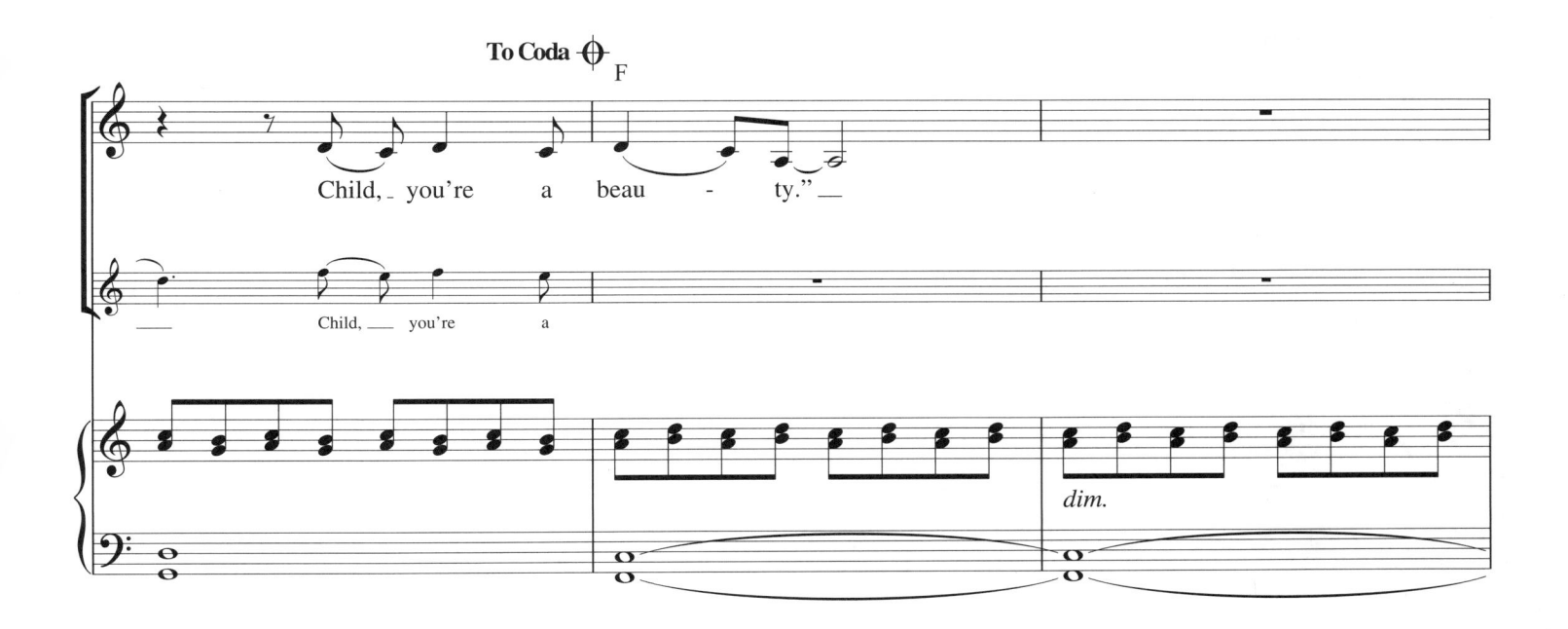

God, it's good—the lov-in'. Ain't it good to-night? You ain't seen noth-in' yet— gon-na {treat / teach} you right. It's just you and me. Child, you're a beau-ty."

(Ah... ah... Child, you're a...)

ILSE: I don't scream, though I know it's wrong. I just play along. I lie there and breathe, lie there and breathe. I wanna be strong, I want the world to find out that you're dreamin' on

Dm7
F5
Am(add2)
me,
me and my "beau - ty,"
Dm7
F5
Am(add2)
add MARTHA:
D.S. al Coda
me and my "beau - ty."
You say all
CODA
F
Add first ENSEMBLE GIRL:
E(add♭6)
beau - ty."
There is a part I can't tell
beau - ty.
Ah,
f

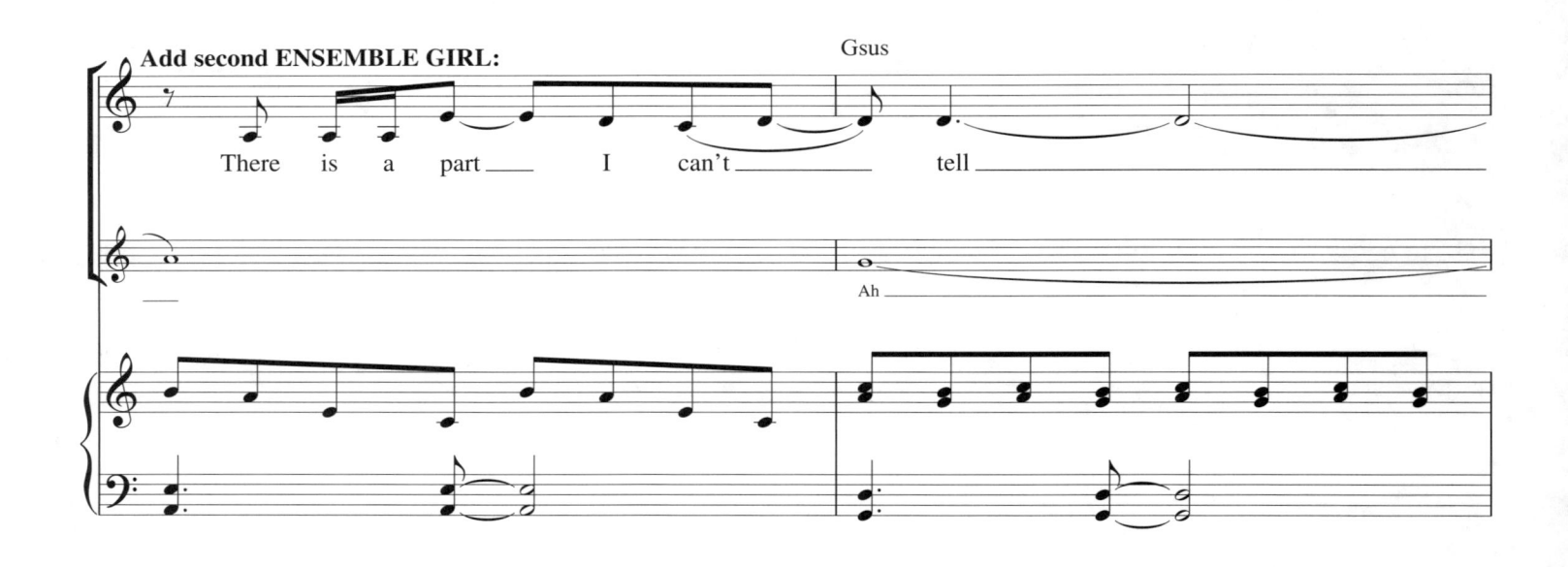

234

'bout the dark I know well.

dark I know well.

Add second ENSEMBLE GIRL:
There is a part I can't tell

Ah

'bout the dark I know well. There is a part I can't

ah

E(add♭6)
Am(add2)
tell 'bout the dark I know well.
ah, dark I know well.
Gsus
There is a part I can't tell
Ah
F
'bout the dark I know well.
ah.

MAMA WHO BORE ME

from *Spring Awakening*

Music by DUNCAN SHEIK
Lyrics by STEVEN SATER

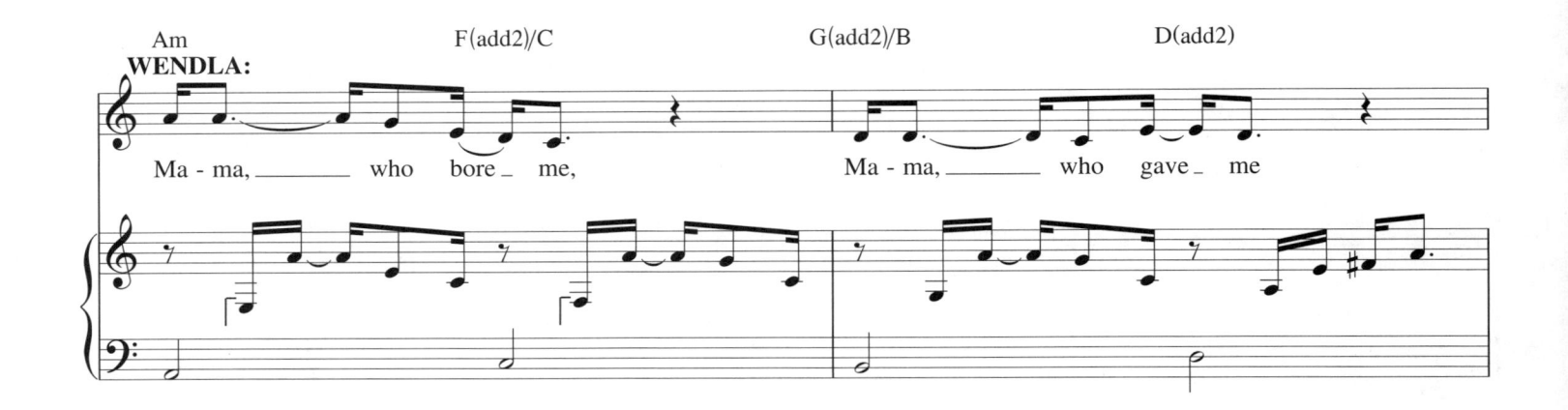

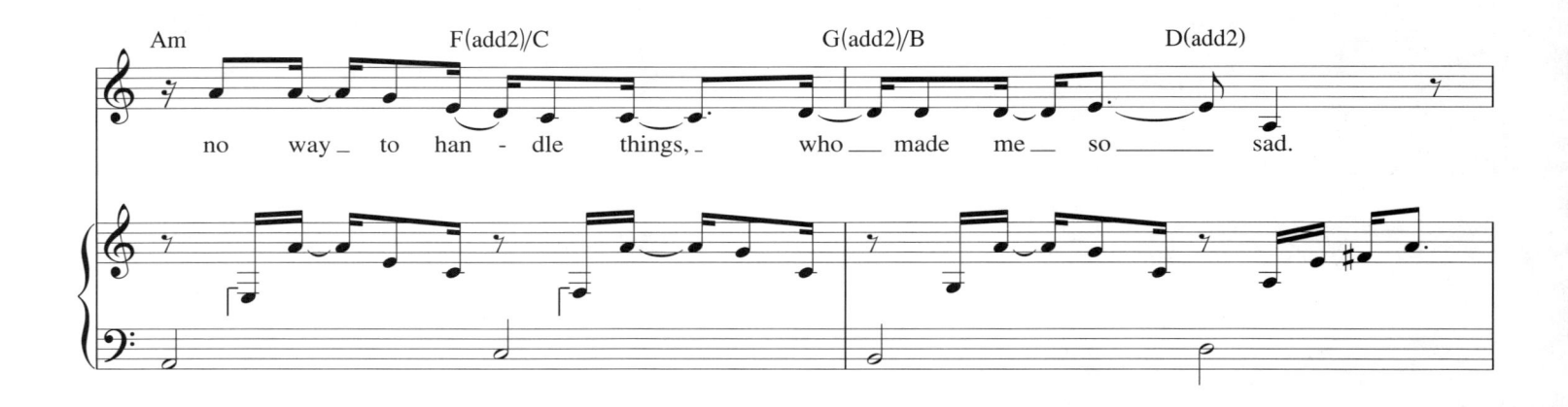

WENDLA:
Mama, who bore me, Mama, who gave me no way to handle things, who made me so sad.
Mama, the weeping, Mama, the angels.

*Copyright © 2006 by Universal Music - Careers, Duncan Sheik Songs, Happ Dog Music and Kukuzo Productions, Inc.
All Rights for Duncan Sheik Songs and Happ Dog Music Administered by Universal Music - Careers
International Copyright Secured   All Rights Reserved*

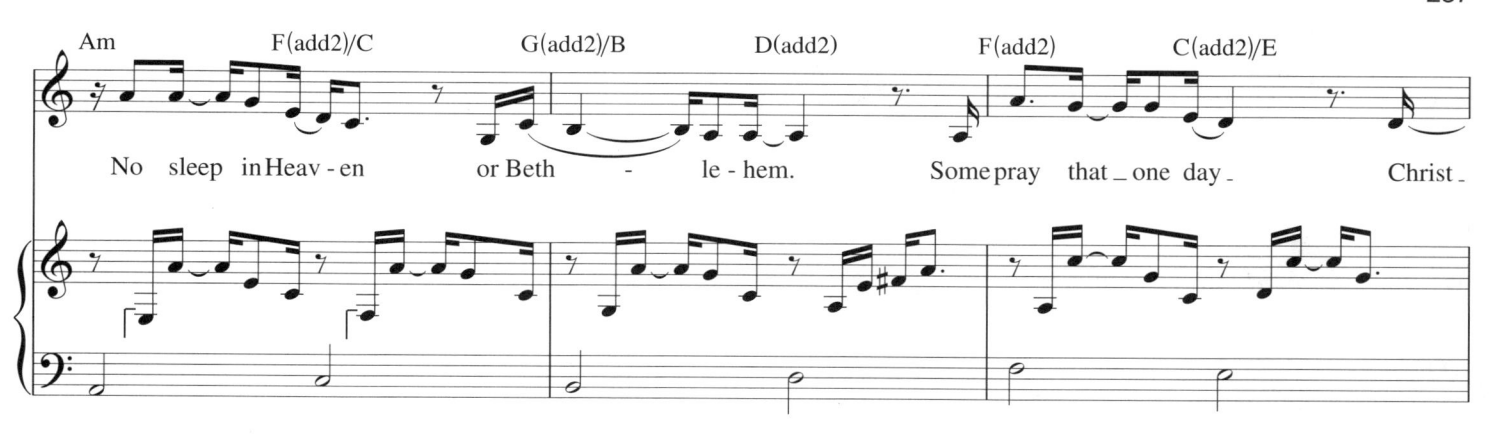

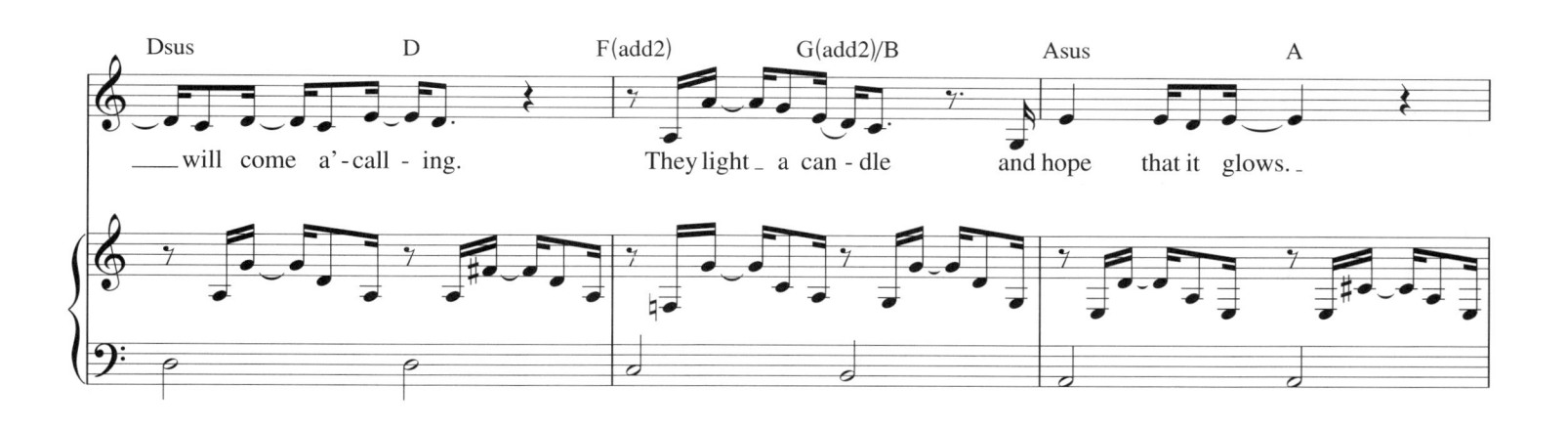

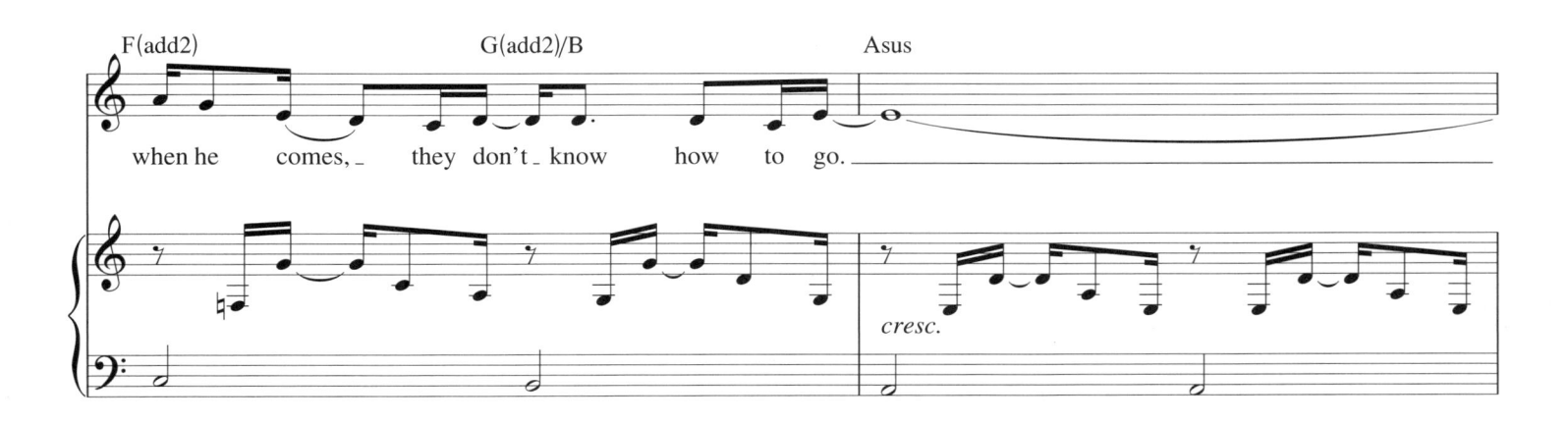

No sleep in Heaven or Bethlehem. Some pray that one day Christ will come a'-calling. They light a candle and hope that it glows. And some just lie there, crying for him to come and find them. But when he comes, they don't know how to go.

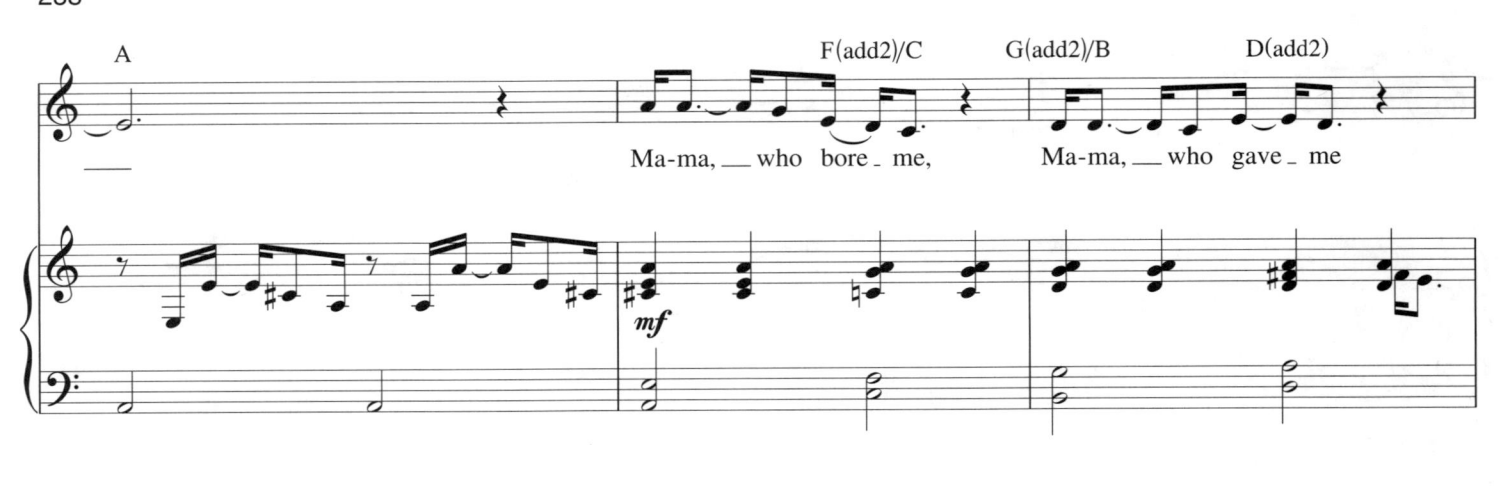

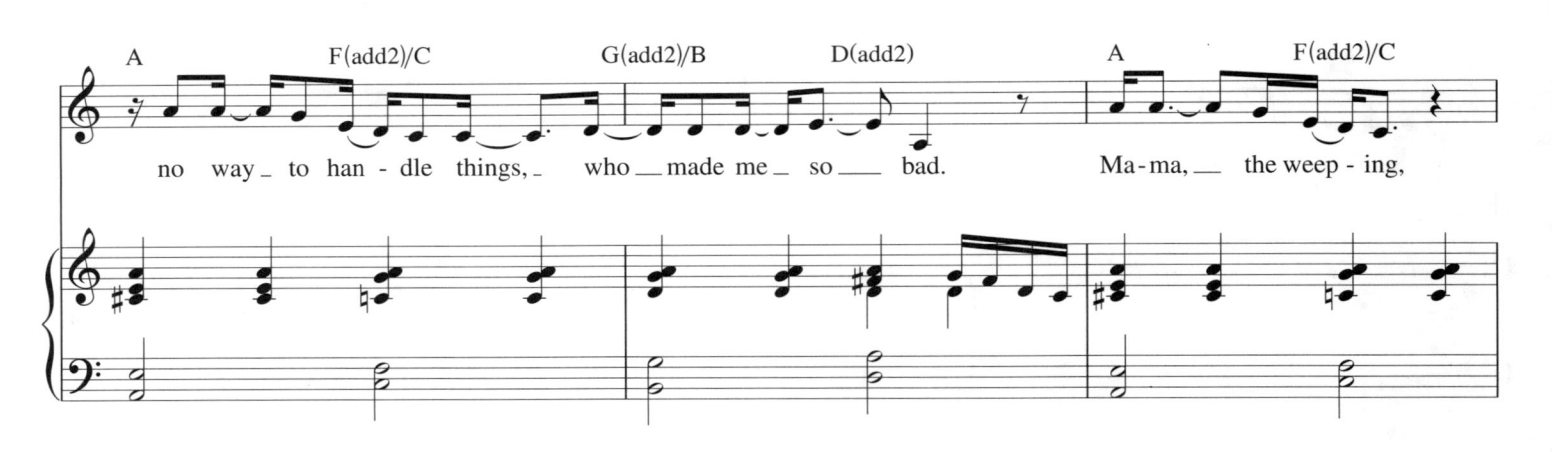

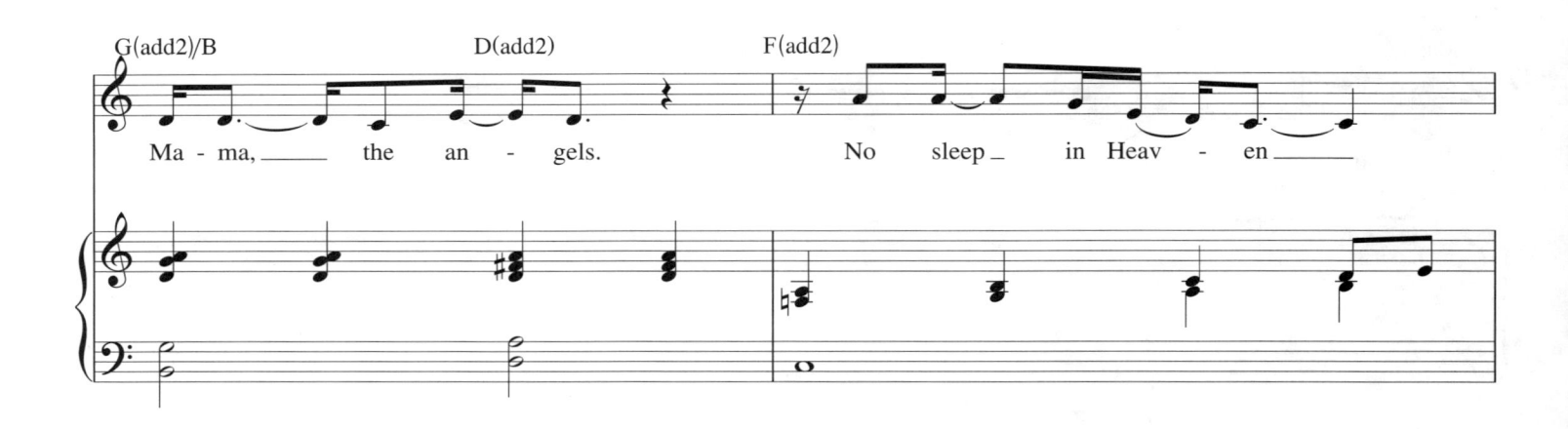

Mama, who bore me, Mama, who gave me no way to handle things, who made me so bad. Mama, the weeping, Mama, the angels. No sleep in Heaven or Bethlehem.

WHERE AM I GOING
from *Sweet Charity*

Music by CY COLEMAN
Lyrics by DOROTHY FIELDS

CHARITY (*spoken before intro begins*): You're damned right I'm going.

Rhythmically

The only trouble is, I don't know where. Where am I go-ing? And what will I find? What's in this grab bag that I call my mind?

Copyright © 1965 Notable Music Company, Inc. and Lida Enterprises
Copyright Renewed
All Rights Administered by Chrysalis Music
All Rights Reserved   Used by Permission

What am I doing alone on the shelf? Ain't it a shame, but no one's to blame but myself! Which way is clear? When you've lost your way year after year. Do I keep falling in love __ for just the kick __ of it, stag-ger-ing through __ the thin and thick __ of it, hat-ing each old __ and ti-red trick __ of it? Know what I am, __ I'm good and sick __ of it! Where am I go - ing? __ Why do I care? __

Run to the Bronx or Wash-ing-ton Square, no mat-ter where I run I meet my-self there, look-ing in-side me. What do I see? An-ger and hope and doubt, what am I all a-bout, and where am I go-ing? You tell me!

Ad lib. in two

Look-ing in-side me, what do I see?

An-ger and hope and doubt, what am I all a-bout, and where am I go-ing?

[*p*] **Freely**

You tell me!

rit.

IF MY FRIENDS COULD SEE ME NOW

from *Sweet Charity*

Music by CY COLEMAN
Lyrics by DOROTHY FIELDS

(spoken): The girls at the ballroom would never believe me in a million years. If they could

Copyright © 1965 Notable Music Company, Inc. and Lida Enterprises
Copyright Renewed
All Rights Administered by Chrysalis Music
All Rights Reserved   Used by Permission

see me now — that little gang of mine, — I'm eating fancy chow and drinking fancy wine. — I'd like those stumble bums to see for a fact — the kind of top drawer, first rate chums I at-tract! All I can say is "Wow-ee" look a where I am___ to-night I land-ed, POW!___ Right in a pot of jam.___ What a set up, ho-ly cow!___ ___ They'd nev-er be-lieve it, if my friends could see me now!___

If they could see me now, my little dusty group. Traips-in' 'round this mil-lion dol-lar chick-en coop! I'd hear those thrift shop cats say:

"Brother! Get her!" Draped on a bedspread made from three kinds of fur! All I can say is: "WOW!" wait 'till the riff and raff see just exactly how he signed this autograph! What a build-up! Holy cow, they'd nev-er be-lieve it, if my friends could see me now!

If they could see me now __ a-lone with Mis-ter V! __ Who's

waiting on me like he was a maitre D! I hear my buddies saying: "Crazy! What gives? Tonight she's living like the other half lives!" To think the highest-brow, which I must say is he, should pick the lowest brow, which there's no doubt is me, what a set up, ho-ly cow!

They'd nev-er be-lieve it!

They'd nev-er be-lieve it! If my friends could see

me now!

YOU'LL BE IN MY HEART
from *Disney Presents Tarzan The Broadway Musical*

Words and Music by
PHIL COLLINS

Tenderly ... *Freely*

KALA: Come stop your cry-ing, it will be al-right. Just take my hand, hold it tight. I will pro-tect you from all a-round you. I will be here, don't you cry.

In tempo

For one so small, you seem so strong.

© 1999 Edgar Rice Burroughs, Inc. and Walt Disney Music Company
All Rights Reserved   Used by Permission

My arms will hold you, keep you safe and warm. This bond be-tween us can't be bro-ken. I will be here, don't you cry. 'Cause you'll be in my heart. Yes, you'll be in my heart from this day on, now and for-ev-er

more.
You'll be in my heart
no mat - ter what they say.
You'll
be here in my heart
al - ways.
Don't lis - ten to him, 'cause what does he know?
We
des - ti - ny calls you, you must be strong.
I
mf

need each oth-er to have, to hold. He'll
may not be with you, but you've got to hold on. They'll

see in time, I know.
see in time, I know.

When know. We'll show them to-geth-er 'cause

you'll be in my heart. Yes, you'll be in my heart from

this day on, __ now __ and __ for-ev-er more.

Oh, __ you'll be __ in my heart no mat-ter what __ they say. You'll be here in __ my __ heart al-ways. __ Al - ways. Al - ways.

dim. *molto rit.* *p*

NOT FOR THE LIFE OF ME
from *Thoroughly Modern Millie*

Music by JEANINE TESORI
Lyrics by DICK SCANLAN

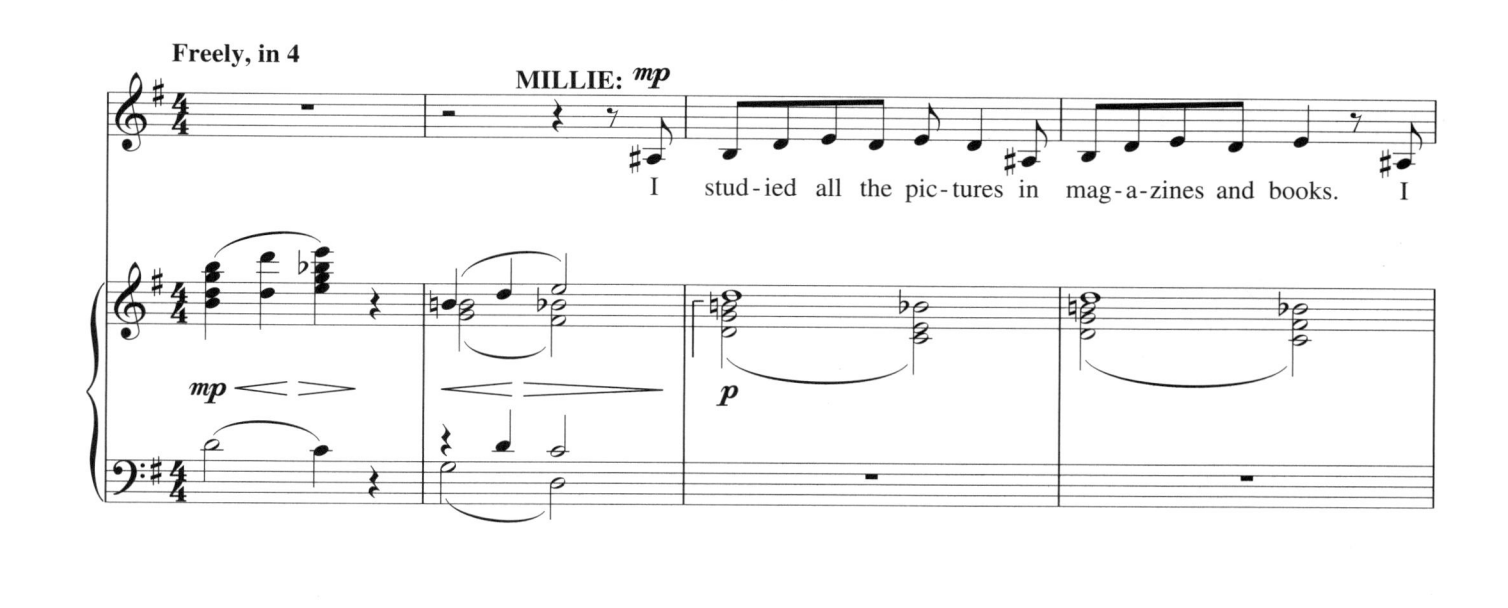

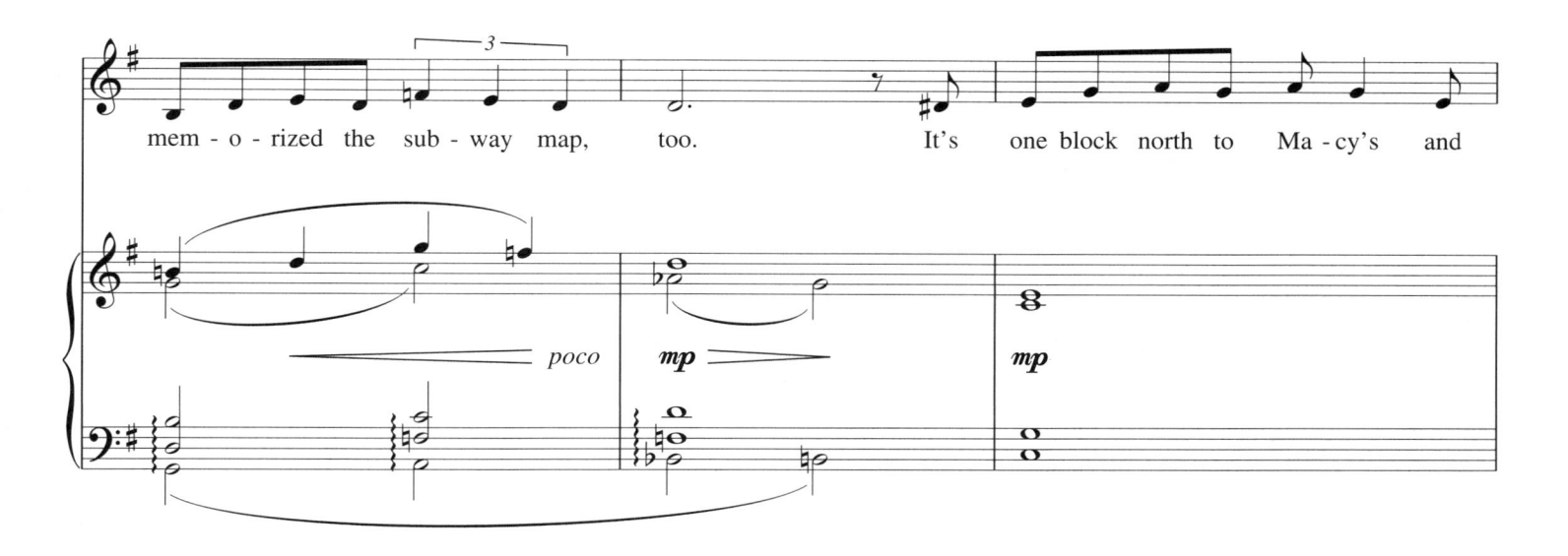

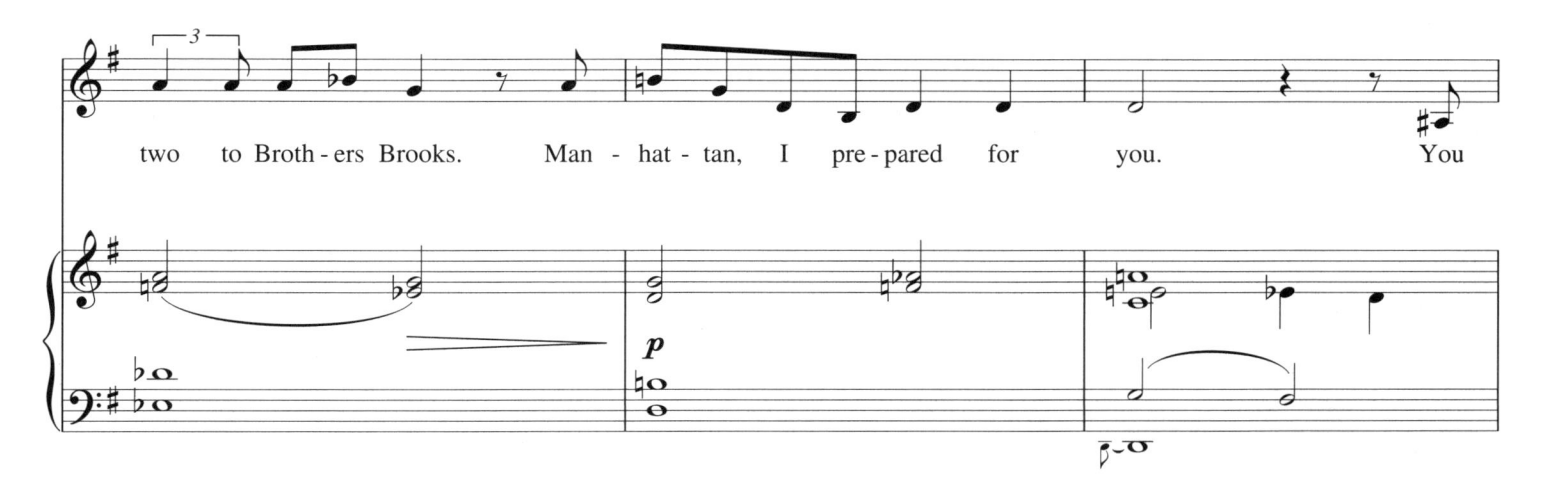

Freely, in 4

MILLIE:
I stud-ied all the pic-tures in mag-a-zines and books. I mem-o-rized the sub-way map, too. It's one block north to Ma-cy's and two to Broth-ers Brooks. Man-hat-tan, I pre-pared for you. You

Copyright © 2001 That's Music To My Ears Ltd. and Thoroughly Modern Music Publishing Co.
International Copyright Secured   All Rights Reserved

certainly are diff-'rent from what they have back home, where nothing's over three stories high, and no one's in a hurry or wants to roam, but I do, though they wonder why. They said I would soon be good and lonely. They said I would sing the homesick blues. So I al - ways have this tic - ket in my poc - ket; a tic - ket home in my poc - ket to do with as I choose.

Slower

Wide Swing - Hot Dixieland

Burn the bridge. Bet the store. Ba - by's com - in' home no more. Not for the life of me. Break the lock. Post my bail.

Done my time I'm out-ta jail. ___ Not for the life of me. A life that's

Più mosso

got-ta be more than a one-light town where the light is al-ways red. ___

Got-ta be more ___ than an old ghost town where the

ghost ain't ev-en dead.

Clap-a-your hands just-a be-cause don't you know that where I am ain't where I was. Not for the life of me. You see I got-ta be more than a

* *On the original cast recording there is a cut from here to **.*

coun-try wife_ mak-in' ba - bies till I croak._

Got-ta be more_ than a lead-ing role_ in a farm-er's

daugh-ter joke!_ Days of yore,_ kind and gen-tle

ask me if I'm sen-ti-men-tal. Not for the life of

me. Boh doh dee oh! Not for the life of, not for the life of, not for the life of me!

COME TO YOUR SENSES

from *tick, tick... BOOM!*

Words and Music by
JONATHAN LARSON

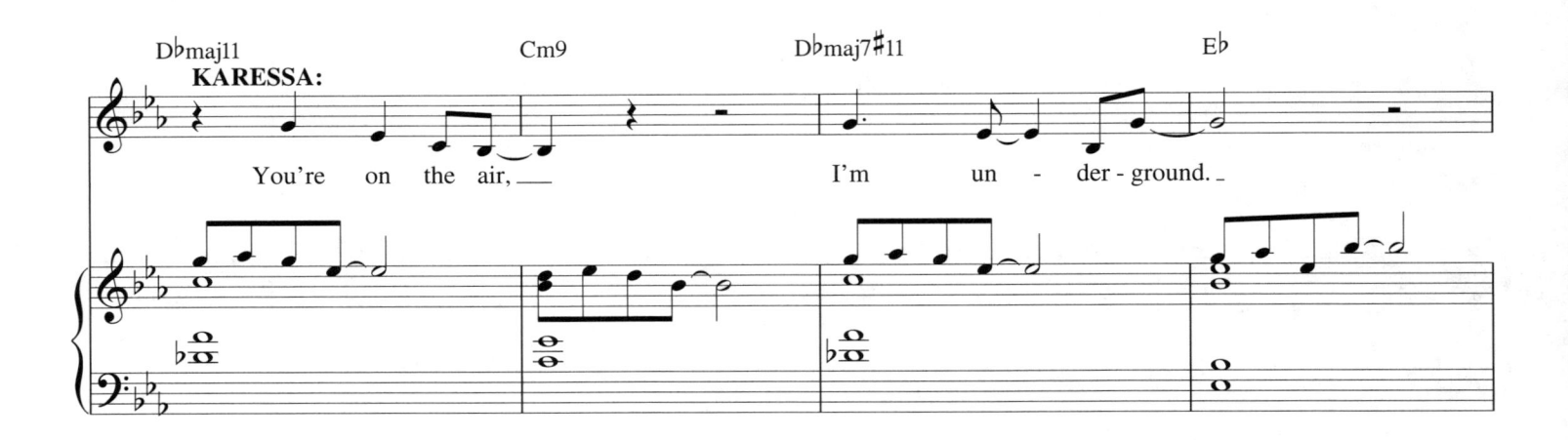

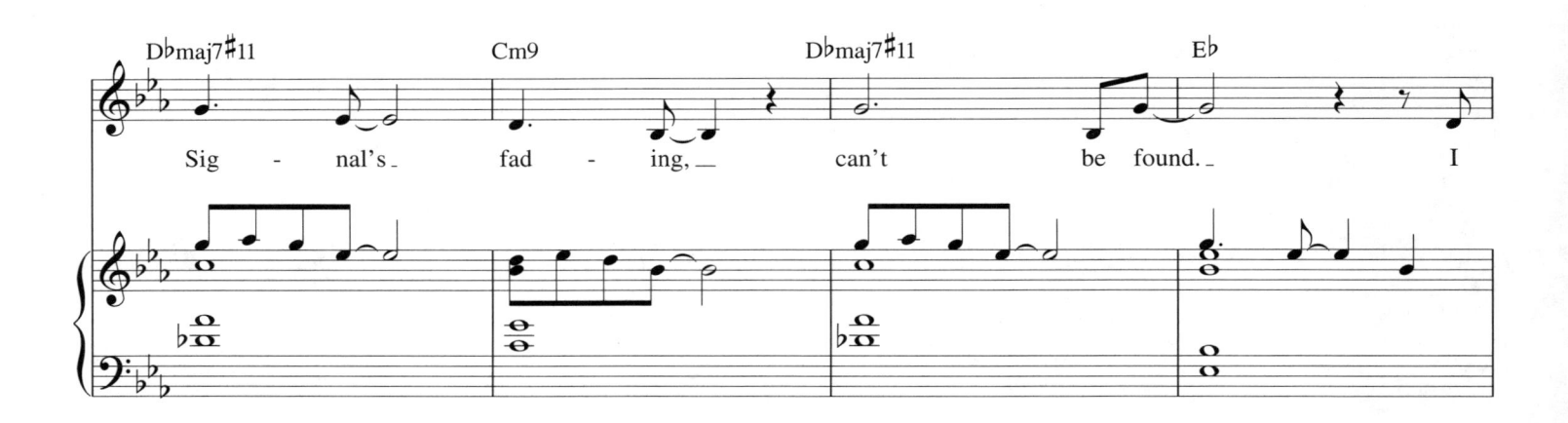

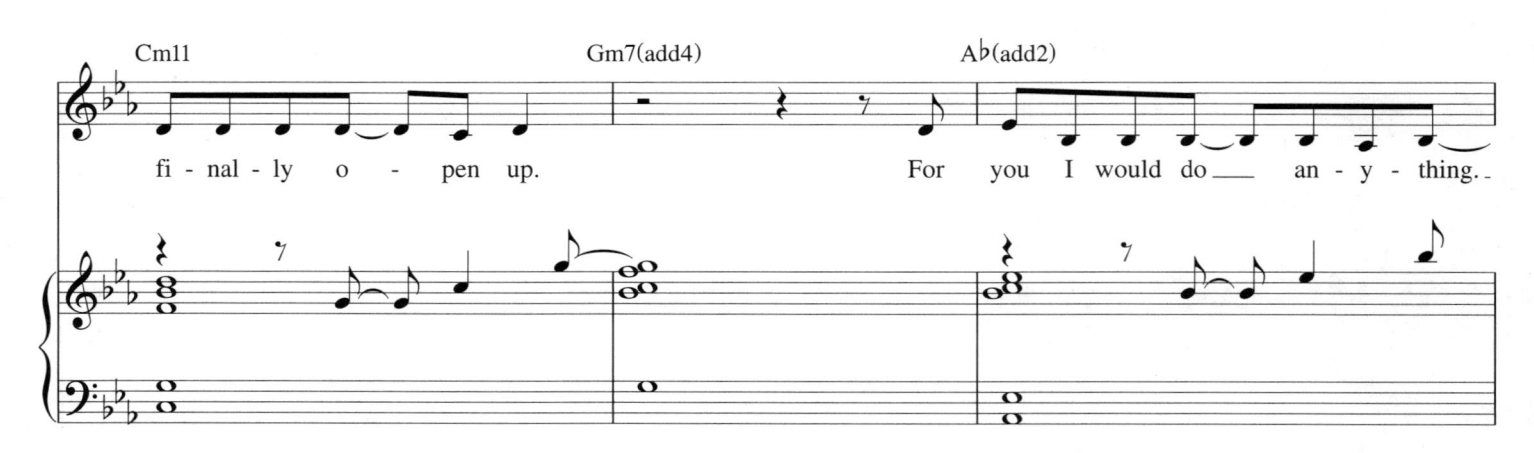

KARESSA: You're on the air, I'm underground. Signal's fading, can't be found. I finally open up. For you I would do anything.

Copyright © 2001 SKEEZIKS LTD. CO.
All Rights Controlled and Administered by UNIVERSAL MUSIC CORP.
All Rights Reserved   Used by Permission

But you've turned off the volume just when I've begun to sing.

Come to your sens - es. De - fens - es are not the way to go, and you know, or at least you knew.

Ev - 'ry thing's strange, you've changed, and I don't know what to do to get through. I don't

Lyrics:

...know what to do. I have to laugh, we sure put on a show. Love is passé in this day and age. How can we expect it to grow? You as the Knight. Me as the Queen.

E♭sus
B♭/D
Cm7(add4)
Gm7(add4)
All I've got to - night is
A♭(add2)
B♭sus
B♭
stat - ic on a screen.
E♭sus2
Gm7
A♭maj9
Come to your sens - es. The fenc - es in - side are not for real if we feel as we did,
mf
a little detached
Cm7
B♭sus
B♭
E♭sus2
Gm7
and I do. Can't you re - call when this all be - gan? It was on - ly

you and me. It was on - ly me ____ and you. ____

But ____ now the air ____ is filled ____ with con -

fu - sion. ____ We've re - placed

care with il - lu - sion. ____ It's cool to ____ be

cold. Nothing lasts anymore. Love becomes disposable. This is the shape of things we can not ignore. Come to your senses. Suspense is fine if you're just an empty image emanating out of a screen.

F(add2)
Am7
B♭sus2
Ba - by, be real, you can feel a - gain You don't need a mu - sic box mel - o - dy to
Dm7
C
B♭sus2
F/A
know what I mean. Deep in my eyes, what do you see?
B♭sus2
Dm
B♭sus2
Deep in my sighs, lis - ten to me. Let the mu -
F/A
B♭sus2
F/A
- sic com - mence from in - side. Not on - ly one sense, but use all five.

Come to your sens - es. Come to your sens - es. Come to your sens - es. Ba - by, come back a - live.

DEFYING GRAVITY
from the Broadway Musical *Wicked*

Music and Lyrics by
STEPHEN SCHWARTZ

Freely, with quiet intensity

ELPHABA:
Something has changed within me, something is not the same. I'm through with playing by the rules of someone else's game. Too late for sec-

-ond guess-ing, too late to go back to sleep

It's time to trust my in-stincts, close my eyes and

Allegro

leap... It's time to try de-fy-

-ing grav-i-ty I think I'll

try de-fy-ing grav-i-ty, and you can't pull me down.

I'm through ac-cept-ing lim-its 'cause some-one says they're so. Some things I can-not change, but 'til

I try, I'll never know. Too long I've been a-fraid of losing love. I guess I've lost. Well, if that's love, it comes at much too high a cost... I'd sooner buy defying grav - i - ty Kiss me good - bye, I'm de-fy-ing grav - i - ty, and you can't pull me down.

Moderato, dreamily

Un - lim - it - ed... My fu - ture is

un - lim - it - ed. And I've just had a vision al - most like a proph - e - cy, I know— It sounds tru - ly cra - zy, and true, the vi - sion's ha - zy... But I swear some - day I'll be up in the sky, de - fy - ing gravity. Flying so high, defying gravity, They'll never pull me down....

So if you care

to find me, look to the western sky
As someone told me lately: ev-'ry-one deserves the chance to fly! And if I'm flying solo, at least I'm flying free To those who'd ground

G♭5/F
D♭/G♭
A♭sus
me, take a mes - sage back from me…
A♭
B♭m7(no5th)
G♭sus2
A♭sus
Tell them how I am de-fy - ing
8va
grav - i - ty I'm fly - ing high de-fy - ing
B♭m7(no5th)
G♭sus2
A♭sus
E♭m/F
Fm7
grav-i-ty, and soon I'll match them in re -
rall.

With determination

nown... And no-bod-y in all of Oz, no Wiz-ard that there is or was is ev-er gon-na bring me down... Ah!...

FOR GOOD
from the Broadway Musical *Wicked*

Music and Lyrics by
STEPHEN SCHWARTZ

Freely

ELPHABA: I'm li-mi-ted, just look at me— I'm li-mi-ted. And just look at you, you can do all I could-n't do, Glin-da... So now it's up to you... *(Spoken:)* for both of us... Now it's up to you.

Tenderly, poco rubato

With pedal

Note: When performed as a solo, sing the top melody line throughout.

Copyright © 2003 Greydog Music
All Rights Reserved   Used by Permission

GLINDA: I've heard it said that people come in-to our lives for a reason, bring-ing some-thing we must learn. And we are led to those who help us most to grow, if we let them, and we help them in re-turn.

Well, I don't know if I be-lieve that's true, But I

know I'm who I am today... because I knew you...

Like a comet pulled from orbit as it passes a sun, like a stream that meets a boulder halfway through the wood, who can say if I've been changed for the better? But because I knew you,

285

I have been changed for good.

ELPHABA: *It well may be that we will never meet again in this lifetime, so let me say before we part: So much of me is made of what I learned from you, you'll be with me like a*

hand-print on my heart. And now what-ev-er way our stor-ies end, I know you have re-writ-ten mine by be-ing my friend... Like a ship blown from its moor-ing by a wind off the sea, like a seed dropped by a sky-bird in a dis-tant wood, who can say— if I've been changed for the bet-ter? But be-cause I knew you...

GLINDA:
Be - cause I knew you...
BOTH:
I have been changed_____ for

Più mosso
ELPHABA:
good... And just to clear the air, I ask for-

give - ness for the things I've done___ you blame me— for.

G♯m7
GLINDA:
B 6
C♯sus C♯/B
F♯/A♯
But then, I guess we know there's blame to share, and
ELPHABA:
and
Emaj7(no3rd)/A
F♯m7(add4)
F♯m7/B
B
B/A
none of it seems to mat-ter an - y - more… Like a com-
none of it seems to mat-ter an - y - more…
rit.
D♭/F
G♭sus2
D♭sus/C♭
D♭
- et pulled from or - bit as it pass - es a sun like a
Like a ship blown from its moor - ing by a wind off the sea,
a tempo

stream that meets a boulder halfway through the wood,

like a seed dropped by a bird in the wood,

Who can say if I've been changed for the better?
Who can say if I've been changed for the better?

I do believe I have been changed for the better... And
I do believe I have been changed for the better...

Gbsus2 Db/F Gbsus2 Db/F Gbsus2 Db/F
be-cause I knew you…
Be-cause I knew you…
Be-cause I knew you…
Be-cause I knew you…
8va
rit poco a poco
Tempo I
Ebm7(no5th) Db/Gb Absus Db5 Db/Gb
I have been changed for
I have been changed for
rit.
Db5 Db/Gb Gb(add2) Ab Db(add2)
good.
good.
rit.

IT'S AN ART
from *Working*

Music and Lyrics by
STEPHEN SCHWARTZ

Verdi-esque (a la "Traviata")

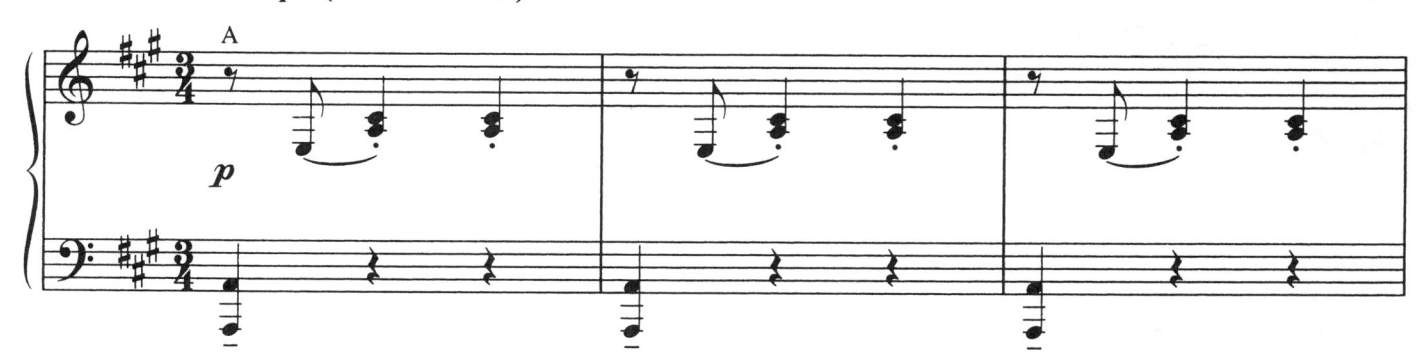

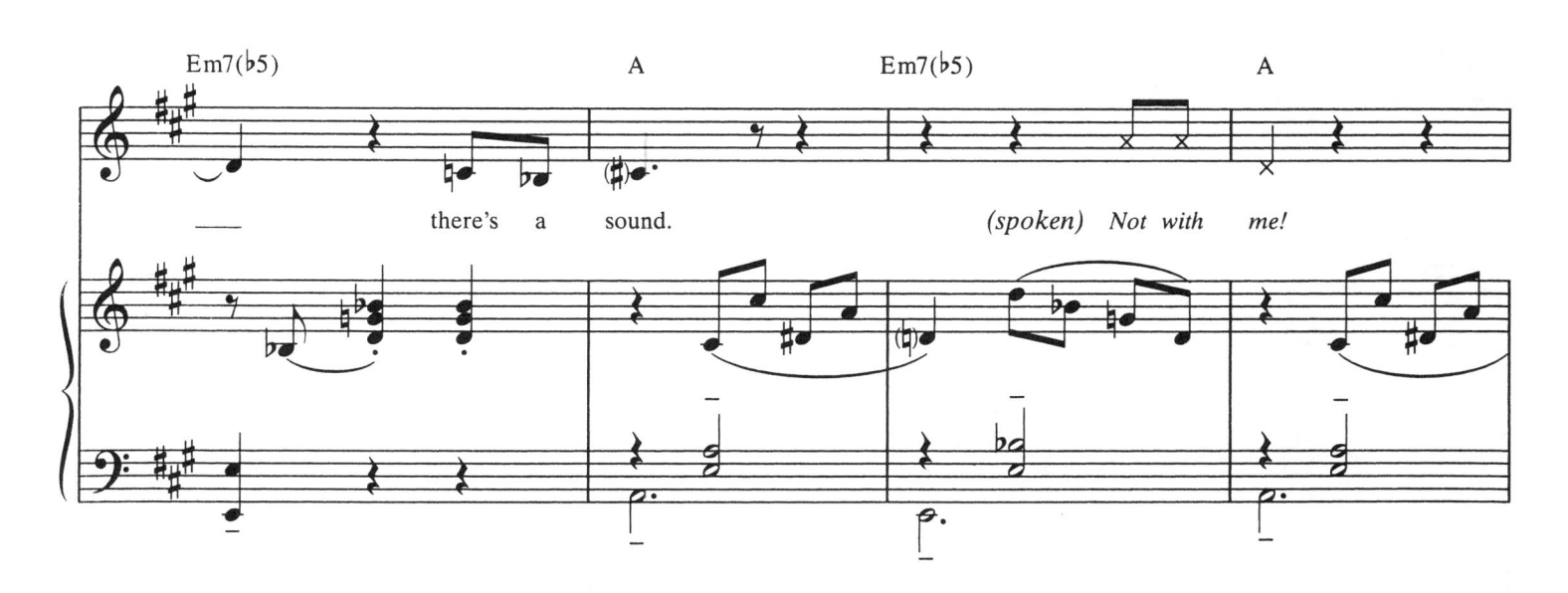

There's some as don't care, when they put down the plate, there's a sound. *(spoken) Not with me!*

Copyright © 1978 Grey Dog Music
Publishing and allied rights for "It's An Art" administered by Williamson Music
International Copyright Secured   All Rights Reserved
www.stephenschwartz.com

(sung) When they move a chair it will scrape with a grate on the ground. *(spoken)* Not with me! *(sung)* I will have my hand right when I place a glass. Notice how I stand right as customers

pass, serve a dem-i-tasse with a ges-ture so gen-tle___ or do it a-gain___ till___ it's near Or-i-en-tal. Da da da da dum da.___ It's an art; It's an art, to be a fine___ waitress, to see that you pleasure each guest. There's a twist to my wrist when I bring your steak in and watch how I take in your liver and bacon, it all needs be stylish and smart.

That's what makes it an art!

I remember one day, as I do now and then, I had shakes. *(spoken)* Down I went!

There with my tray full of coffees and

cor-dials and cakes-- *(spoken)* Down I___ went!

(sung) But I kept my poise, not one guest__ heard me fall.__

Nev-er made a noise, *(spoken)* Not one noise, *(sung)* food and all.

If you have to crawl, you give 'em__ what they like. You

carry___ your tray like it's al-most bal-let-like.___

La la da dum da da___ da da___ da da da da da dum. It's an art!___ It's an art!___ to

be a fine___ wait-ress-- each ev'-ning I treas-ure___ the

test. Like to-night was a fight 'cause they hi-red this bus-boy— this hair-all-a-muss boy— and guests heard him cuss— boy, did we have a quick "heart-to-heart!" E-ven that was— an art.

Tips! Hah! Tips are important to people like captains and barmen! *(spoken)* To them it's a tip, see? To me, *(sung)* I'm a gypsy! Just toss me a coin and I suddenly feel like I'm Carmen!

F♯7/E
E♭7
F♯7/E
F
F7
molto rall.
mp
So
f
p
molto rall.
Tempo I°
A
A/C♯
B♭/E
B♭
A
on through the ul - cer, the back - ache, the hot sweat-y feet,
3
Em7(♭5)
A
E7(♭5)
A
C♯m7
(spoken)
on you go. Through: "Is your knife dull, sir?" and

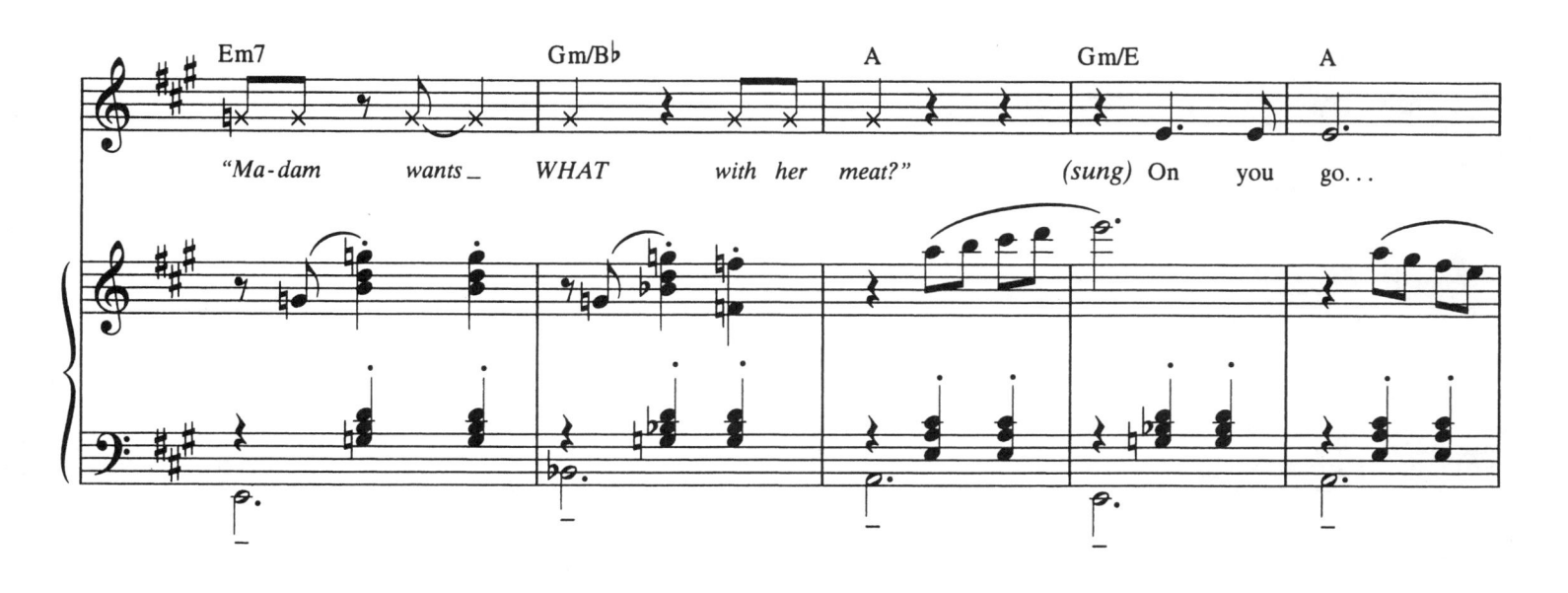

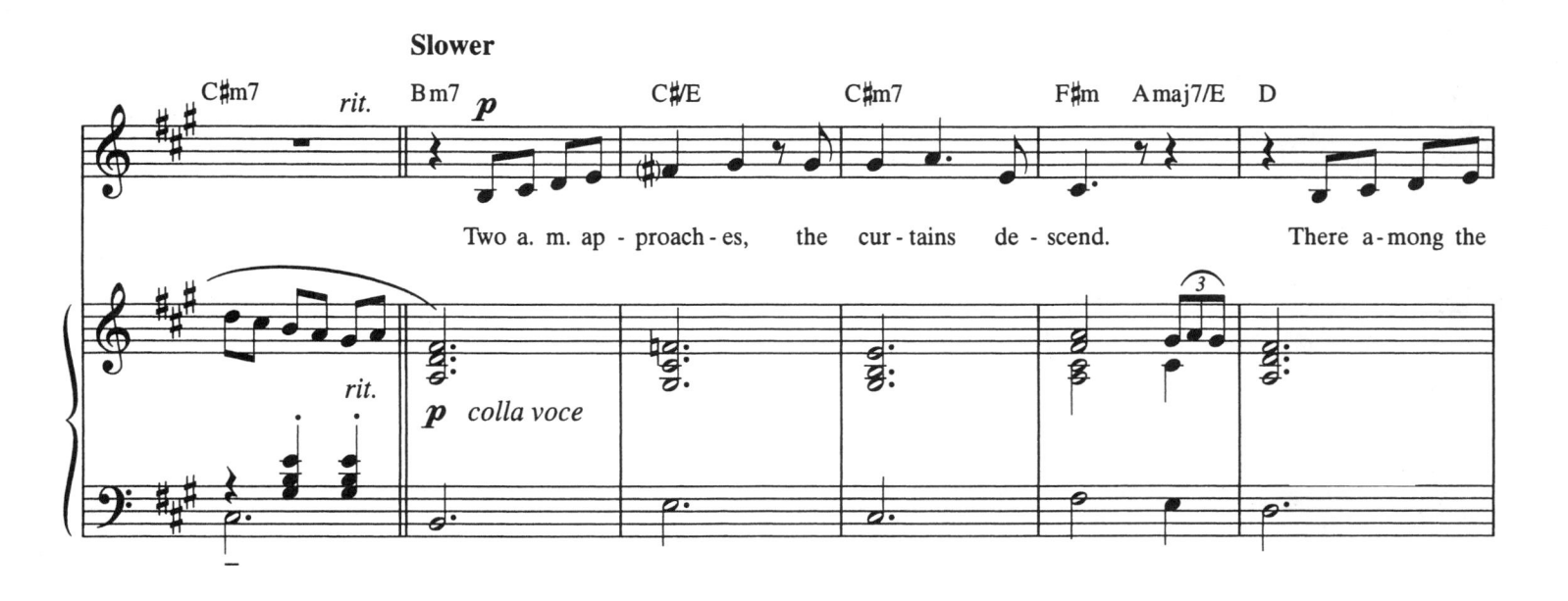

301

"Madam wants _ WHAT with her meat?" *(sung)* On you go...

Two a.m. approaches, the curtains descend. There among the roaches, my act's at an end. Ev'ry night I tend to find _ myself crying. There's no work so trying or so satisfying!

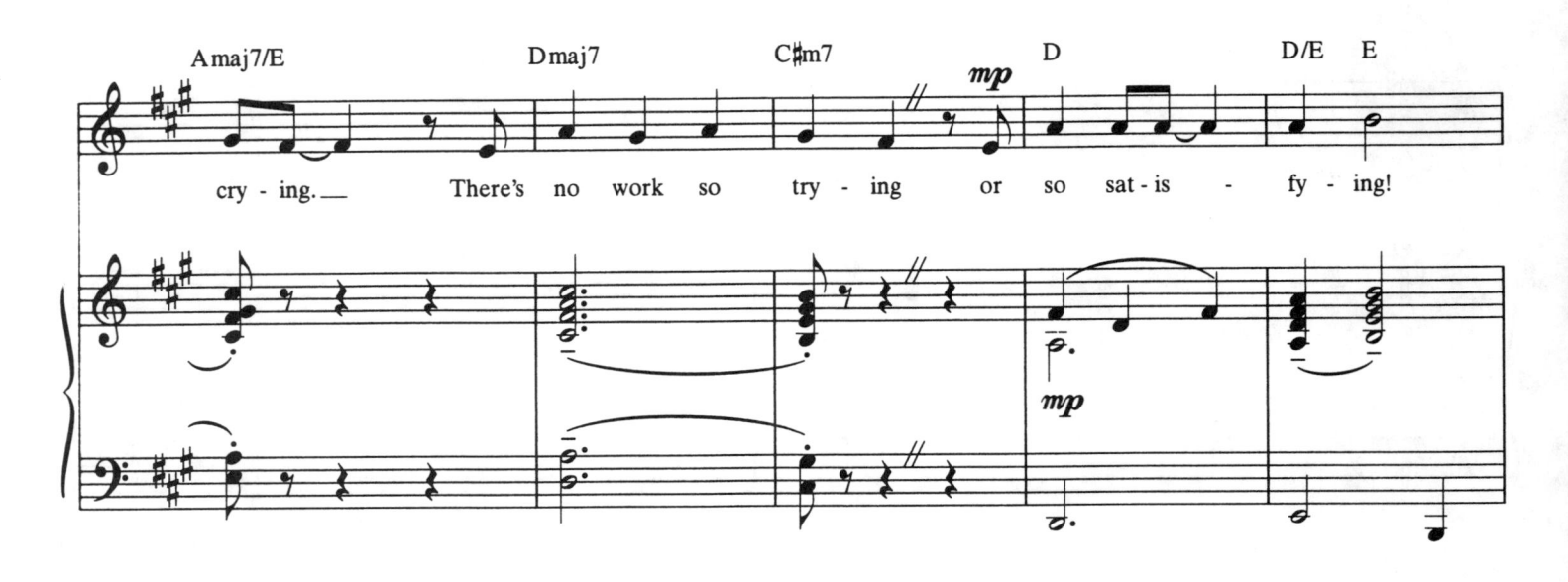

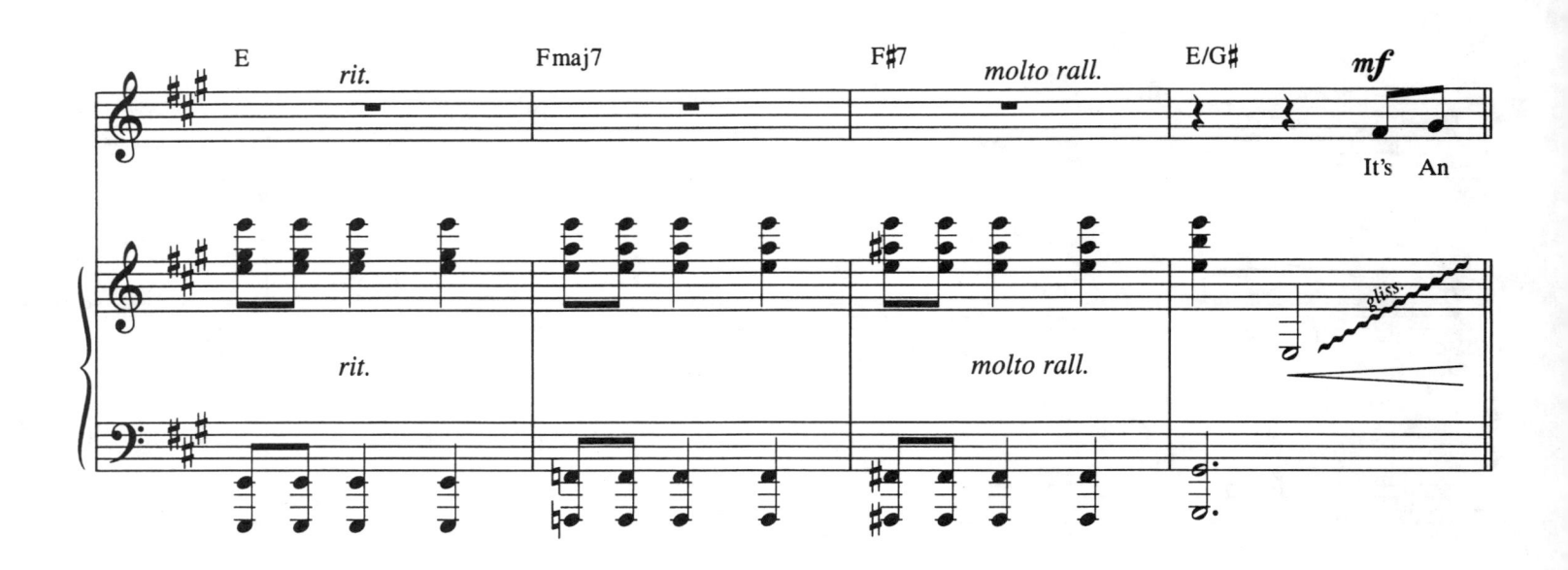

It's An Art! It's An Art! To be a great waitress, to do without

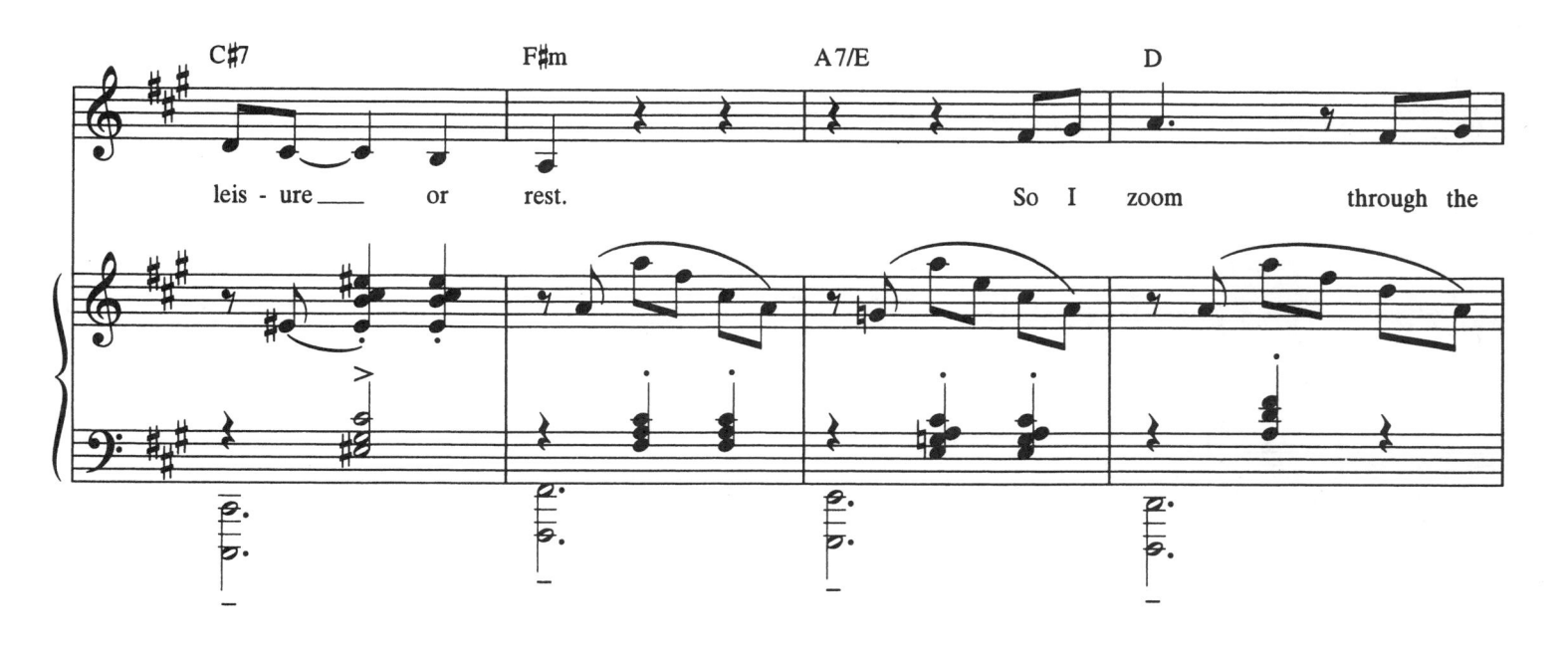

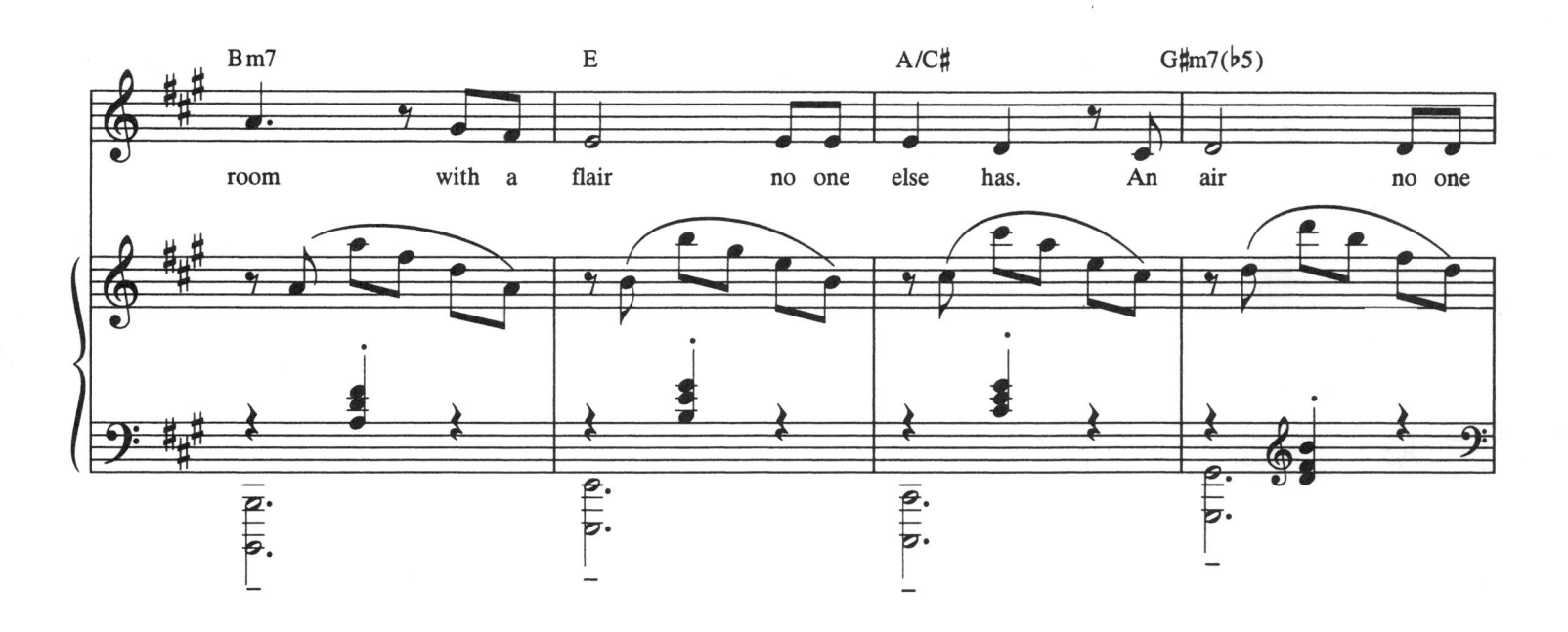

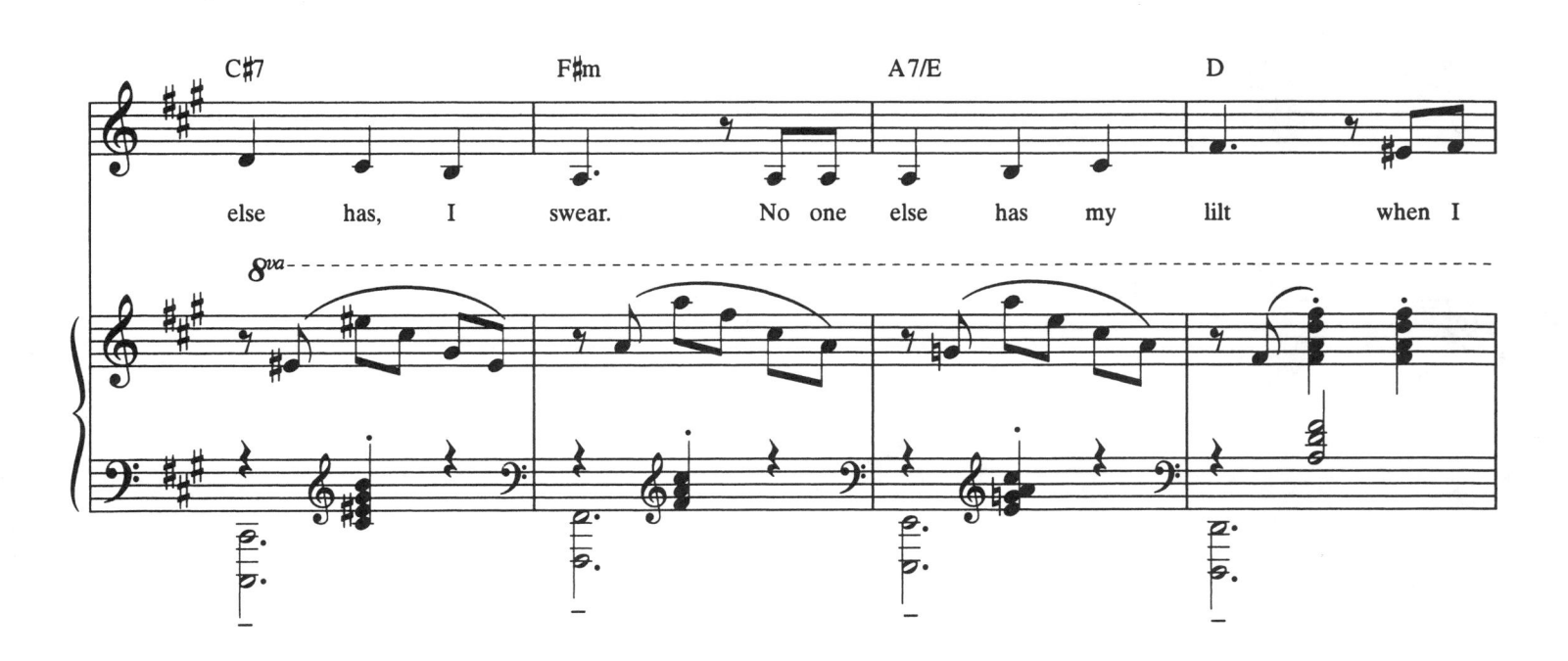

leis-ure___ or rest. So I zoom through the room with a flair no one else has. An air no one else has, I swear. No one else has my lilt when I

say, "A la carte." You can see it

gives me a glow. Ev-'ry-time I

prove I'm a pro. May-be I'm not

quite Mich-ael-an-ge-lo, _____ but I'm not just a wait-ress, I'm a one _____ wom-an _____ show. _____

LIFE IS
from *Zorba*

Words by FRED EBB
Music by JOHN KANDER

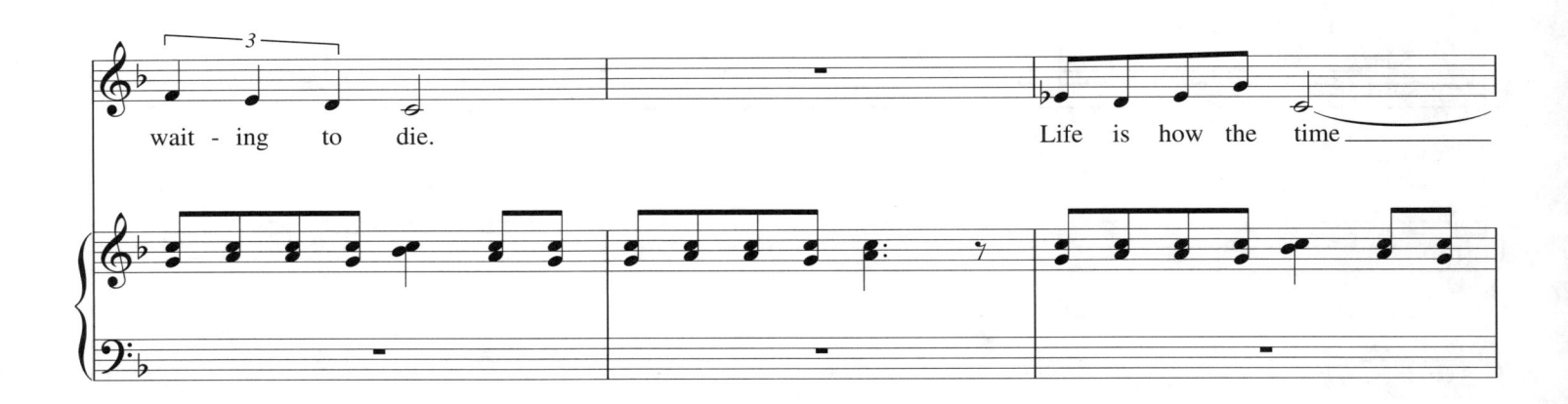

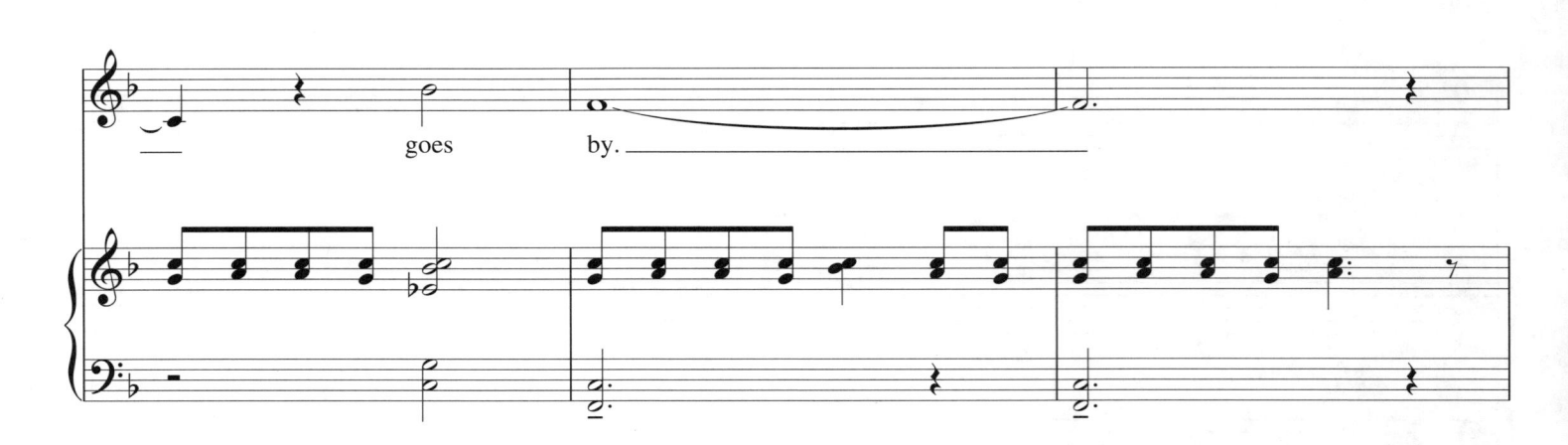

Moderato

pp

LEADER: Life is what you do while you're wait-ing to die. Life is how the time goes by.

Copyright © 1968 by Alley Music Corp. and Trio Music Company
Copyright Renewed
International Copyright Secured   All Rights Reserved
Used by Permission

Life is where you wait

while you're wait - ing to leave.

Life is where you grin and grieve.

Having if you're lucky, wanting if you're not. Looking for the ruby underneath the rot. Hungry for the pilaf in someone else's pot. But that's the only choice you've got!

Life is where you stand just be - fore you are flat.
Life is on - ly that, Mis - ter. Life is sim - ply that, Mis - ter,
that and noth - ing more than that.
p
p

Life is what you feel till you can't feel at all.
mf
Life is where you fly and
fall.
f
Run-ning for the shel - ter na - ked in the snow.
mf

Learn-ing that a tear drops an-y-where you go. Find-ing it's the mud that makes the ros-es grow. But that's the on-ly choice you know.

Life is what you do while you're wait-ing to die.

Rubato
This is how the time goes *colla voce*

A tempo
by.

accel. e cresc. poco a poco

accel.